The Life
and Hard Times of
a Korean Shaman

The Life and Hard Times of a Korean Shaman

OF TALES AND THE TELLING OF TALES

LAUREL KENDALL

UNIVERSITY OF HAWAII PRESS
HONOLULU

Printed in the United States of America

93 92 91 90 89 88 5 4 3 2 1

Library of Congress Cataloging-in-Publication Data

Kendall, Laurel.
The life and hard times of a Korean Shaman.

Bibliography: p.
Includes index.
1. Shaman—Korea (South) 2. Women—Korea (South)—Social conditions I. Title.
BL2236.S5K45 1988 299'.57 87–19152
ISBN 0–8248–1136–4
ISBN 0–8248–1145–3 (pbk.)

To my parents,
Henry and Ramona Kendall

Contents

Acknowledgments ix

ONE The Storyteller 1
TWO A Tale of Deceit and a Tale of Kam'ak Mountain 18
THREE Born in an Unlucky Hour 31
FOUR War Stories and a Meeting with the Mountain God 47
FIVE Buddha Ties 68
SIX The Reluctant Bride 85
SEVEN Old Ghosts and Ungrateful Children 101
EPILOGUE 1985 120

Notes 129
Glossary 139
Bibliography 147
Index 153

Acknowledgments

This book is the product of a long gestation. My initial fieldwork in Korea in 1977 and 1978 was made possible by fellowships from the Institute for International Education (Fulbright) and the Social Science Research Council, as well as by a grant from the National Science Foundation. I began to work with Yongsu's Mother's story during my tenure as a National Institute of Mental Health Post-Doctoral Research Fellow at the University of Hawaii, where I benefited from George Simpson's multidisciplinary seminar on biography. A grant from the Eppley Foundation for Research allowed me to return to Korea in 1985 to complete this project.

Clarissa Wilbur typed the manuscript and Charlotte Boynton, Chung-moo Choi, and Carol Gelber gave it thoughtful readings. Carol provided expert editorial assistance and Chung-moo saved me from some egregious errors of translation. The staff of the University of Hawaii Press helped to make this manuscript a better book. I alone am responsible for its shortcomings.

It would be presumptuous of me to thank the person most responsible for this book. It is Yongsu's Mother's story.

ONE

The Storyteller

> When . . . one reads of a witch being ducked, of a woman possessed by devils, of a wise woman selling herbs, or even of a very remarkable man who had a mother, then I think we are on the track of a lost novelist, a suppressed poet, of some mute and inglorious Jane Austen, some Emily Brontë who dashed her brains out on the moor or mopped and mowed about the highways crazed with the torture that her gift put her to.
>
> —Virginia Woolf, *A Room of One's Own*

The woman who tells her life in the following pages is a Korean shaman, one who invokes the gods and ancestors, speaks with their voice, and claims their power to interpret dreams and visions. If neither a lost novelist nor an unrecognized poet (and who can say what she might have been?), the woman is a gifted storyteller. She, herself, might call that gift a curse, the force of a destined shaman's strange, bitter, and wondrous history. She recounts that history in tales that are sometimes angry, often melodramatic, usually touched with humor, and polished for having been told and retold in the company of other women. Her story is neither a smoothly seamed autobiography nor a sequence of archetypal stages in a Korean life cycle, but a series of connected and sometimes contradictory complaints, cautionary tales, and entertainments fashioned by a distinctive voice in the world of their telling. It is this twofold experience, of both her tales and her telling of tales, that I shall attempt to record and convey.

In 1976, early in my dissertation research, I was introduced to a vivacious and witty *mansin* whom I will call Yongsu's Mother. This lean, animated woman with a forthright gaze and ready laugh became my teacher and confidante. Elsewhere, I have described the circumstances of our first meeting.

> She was at work in her shrine, chanting as she waved a struggling white chicken over a tray of offering food while a tiny gray-haired woman rubbed her hands in supplication. . . . Relieved of her ritual duties, Yongsu's Mother suggested a game of flower cards with a round of cheap

> rice wine as the stake. She proceeded to coach me, peering over my shoulder, telling me which card to set down, and cautioning me in a stage whisper that other players were peeking at my hand. The card game set the tone of our working relationship, a relationship characterized by Yongsu's Mother's nonstop flow of information and advice, her patience, her well-intended but occasionally overbearing desire to protect and coddle me, and her mischievous sense of humor. (Kendall 1985:51)

I spent some portion of nearly every day that I was in the field with Yongsu's Mother, either accompanying her to rituals in client households, or observing divination sessions and minor rituals in her own home. When there were neither rituals nor clients, I would ask her to clarify points or answer the multitude of questions that had occurred to me while I transcribed my most recent batch of field notes. Yongsu's Mother loves to talk; her language is clear and fluid, accompanied by graphic gestures and tragicomic expressions. The book that I eventually wrote is better for her sharp observations and sense of humor.

Her expressed reason for helping me was that some awful fate must have cast me adrift, far from my native land, and that misfortune was a bond between us. Also, Yongsu's Mother wanted company; she was frankly bored and lonely sitting at home, waiting for clients while her son was off at school. Some of her boundless enthusiasm for conversation could be satisfied in talking to the anthropologist; she had interesting things to say and I attempted to record every word. In a region much visited by Korean ethnologists and folklorists, it may have been a mark of distinction for a relatively young shaman to have a scholar, albeit a young scholar, in tow.[1]

Between us, we evolved a discourse that bridged the world of the anthropologist and the world of the shaman. She was my teacher and I was her student. I learned in the manner of an apprentice *mansin*, going around to *kut* and gradually building up a store of lore and precedent. In her eyes, my expanding knowledge of the gods in her shrine implied a deepening obligation, theirs to help me succeed, and mine to offer periodic tribute; I ultimately acquired my Ph.D. through the will of the gods and became a success story told to other clients. For my part, I saw in Yongsu's Mother a shrewd capacity for observation and a tolerant curiosity about the world and situations beyond her experience. She might have made an excellent anthropologist but, then, she is a successful shaman.

It is not unusual for an anthropologist to describe a relationship with a wise informant by academic analogy, to hold seminars with a Ndembu philosophy don (Turner 1960), or, upon meeting the shaman informant of one's own graduate student, to discuss that student's apprenticeship "as two teachers who are addressing the progress of a doctoral candidate" (Jaques Maquet in Peters 1981:1). Conversely, the informant may find a satisfactory analogy in becoming a classificatory "aunt," "mother," or "grandmother" to the anthropologist (Blackman 1982:viii; Shostak 1981:39; Zempleni 1977:91) or in taking the anthropologist as an apprentice (Sharon 1978; Peters 1981). But Yongsu's Mother also entered into the spirit of my analogy, intrigued that the activities of a shaman could thus be cast in an aura of scholarly respectability. I would like to think that the prospect of playing honored teacher to a female student amused and pleased her. We agreed that we would each rather pursue our respective careers, however demanding, than sit home all day, heavyhearted.

Because I was more immediately interested in what shamans do than who they are, I did not initially seek a detailed account of Yongsu's Mother's life. Nevertheless, in our many discussions Yongsu's Mother would often use bits and pieces of her own experience to illustrate a point: why she unfailingly makes a mountain pilgrimage or scrupulously honors the death anniversary of her husband's first wife, why she keeps a tiny Buddha statue among the larger images in her shrine, or why her own mother is so often possessed by her Body-Governing God.

As a destined shaman, wondrous things have happened to Yongsu's Mother. The Mountain God's intercession had saved her life during the Korean War. Divine beings brought her a bowl of healing water once in a dream when she was seriously ill. When she was down on her luck, the gods lifted her up and chose her for a shaman. But with the rough fate of a destined shaman, many awful things have happened to her as well. Even her birth hour was unlucky. Father, lover, matchmaker, and husband had all deceived her. Her stepchildren gave her no peace. "When you understand all that has happened to me, Tallae, you will think about it in America and your tears will flow." That was what she said when, one day, she seized the initiative and determined to tell me the story of her life.

I was sympathetic and gave her my undivided attention, wrestling with each fresh assault of Korean language. She knew that some of her vivid prose was lost on me, but there was my tape recorder, silent scribe and resolute witness to her story. Years later, after completing a dissertation and preparing a book, I returned to my tapes and transcripts of Yongsu's Mother's life. With leisure, patience, and a supply of dictionaries, I filled in what I had missed, hurt for her again, marveled anew at her feistiness, and giggled at her comic imagery, as she had intended.

Yongsu's Mother's tales—of poverty, war, forced marriage, and divine possession—are sufficiently engrossing to stand on their own merits. (Readers primarily interested in her story may proceed to chapter 2.) As a record of an otherwise unknown Korean woman's life and as a personal account of life in an older, poorer Korea, Yongsu's Mother's story fulfills the common justifications for recording a life history, oral history, or ethno-biography, but this presentation should serve some other purposes as well. I am in sympathy with those who have urged us to return the individual to anthropology, to consider the manner in which living men and women experience and articulate, sometimes idiosyncratically, the symbolic constructs and ritual systems we present as ethnographic generalizations (Crapanzano 1980; Obeyesekre 1981; Watson and Watson-Franke 1985; Zempleni 1977). Like many other anthropologists, I am dissatisfied with traditional presentations of life history material or, rather, find them too restrictive a frame for the life at hand. Yongsu's Mother does not live an archetypal life; she does not stand for all Korean women, or even, despite some common themes, for all Korean shamans. She does, however, offer personal insights on the religious consciousness of both women and shamans. We learn how one articulate ritual specialist weaves an appropriate idiom, a mountain god or an unquiet soul, into a personal parable and how, having done so, she presents her tale to the audience at hand. I am interested in the fit of Yongsu's Mother the storyteller to Yongsu's Mother the shaman, in her use of dreams, divinations, stories, and healing rituals, to explain and reconcile her own unique ghosts and in how, on this authority, she makes sense of the dreams and stories of others. In a few instances I offer my own experiences to illustrate the bond between shaman, gods, and client. Finally, I would transmit Yongsu's Mother's tales in a manner that suggests both her skill as author and performer and the reflexive experience of hearing, seeing, and remembering, rather than merely recording her story.

Shamans and Other Korean Women

The events that I shall describe transpired, for the most part, in 1977 and 1978 in a place I call "Enduring Pine Village," a settlement of 136 houses on the periphery of Seoul. At that time the Republic of Korea was on the verge of its current status as a Newly Industrialized Country (NIC), and the village reflected a changing rural economy. Buses running along paved roads connected the village to the market town and the capital. Traditional straw roofs had been replaced by slate tile or corrugated metal, and several of these new roofs boasted television antennae. Rice production for subsistence and surplus was no longer the most significant means of livelihood; seventy households, more than half the total, did not grow rice, although they might own or rent vegetable plots and raise livestock. Some of the village men worked at the local military installations or in the town as semiskilled laborers—taxi drivers, factory workers, carpenters, and stone masons. Two men from the village took contracts as drivers for a Korean construction project in Saudi Arabia. By the villagers' own definition, their village was not "real country." The relative prosperity of this community in both recent and traditional times, when it was an administrative seat located at an important crossroads, fostered an elaborate tradition of shaman ritual.

In 1977 Yongsu's Mother lived in a small dark house by the side of the paved road, so close to the road that the roar of passing trucks has been immortalized in my tape recordings. The aged Brass Mirror Mansin, who considered Yongsu's Mother an upstart, referred contemptuously to "that one by the roadside." Like most other village houses, Yongsu's Mother's corrugated metal roof had its television antenna. The television was a recent acquisition, and Yongsu's Mother was particularly fond of costumed historical dramas where greedy and corrupt officials, in antique dress, recalled the machinations of some of the gods in her pantheon.

Sliding wooden doors, their ill-fitting glass panes glued over with large paper snowflakes, shielded the interior of Yongsu's Mother's house from the road. Walls and roof enclosed a small dirt floor and wooden platform, a dark and narrow approximation of the inner courtyard and veranda which are, in traditional country homes, bright, breezy, and open to sunlight. The shrine, to the right of this entrance space, held printed and painted pictures of Yongsu's Mother's gods, plaster Buddha images, and an assortment of metal offering bowls, incense pots, and candlesticks.[2] A small kitchen, in a corner behind the shrine and beside the inner room, was strategically situated so that the heat generated by cooking fuel could be channeled through flues to the inner room and, only occasionally, to the shrine. In the dead of winter, the shrine was excruciatingly cold. Lattice and paper doors behind the wooden floor opened onto the inner room, the warmest and most cheerful section of the house, the place where mother and son actually lived. In addition to the television set and Yongsu's desk and bookshelf, there were two large wardrobe cabinets and a dressing table, covered with bottled cosmetics and lotions, the first evidence of Yongsu's Mother's financial success as a *mansin.* Since going to *kut* meant dressing up, she was more often well groomed and painted than her village neighbors. My casual approach to makeup has never ceased to exasperate her.

Garbed in the red robes of an antique general or wielding the Spirit Warrior's halbard as she drives malevolent forces from her path, Yongsu's Mother claims an imposing presence. Even in everyday dress and sprawling comfortably on the heated floor of her own home, she speaks with authority. By virtue of the powerful gods who possess her, she can summon up divination visions and probe the source of a client's misfortunes, exorcise the sick and chronically unlucky, remove ill humors from those who have difficulty finding mates, and coax a reluctant birth spirit into an infertile womb. The professional shaman makes the gods and ancestors a vivid presence in the home; she spots them in her visions and gives them voice in trance. In *kut,* her most elaborate ritual, she garbs herself in their costumes and in their person scolds, banters, advises, and commiserates with the mortal members of household and community. Like Yongsu's Mother, most Korean *mansin* are women and they minister most immediately to a female clientele. The few men who claim the shaman's powers perform in women's clothing, down to the long silken pantaloons that they wear under their slips.

There is logic, or at least convenience, in the shaman's gender, since women represent their households in the shaman's shrine when they suspect that angry gods or restless ancestors are the root cause of serious or prolonged misfortune. Their visits to the shrine are an extension of other sacred duties. Within the home, women make offerings *(kosa)* to the household gods and, although men conduct the formal rites of ancestor worship *(chesa),* women deal with the restless and potentially dangerous dead. The *mansin* provides a direct link between her clients and their household gods and ancestors. Through divination and the visions she finds in trance, she determines the source of present trouble. If a housewife suspects that spirits lurk behind a nagging illness or a run of bad luck, she consults a *mansin* and has her perform a divination. The housewife may go to her own "regular" *(tan'gol) mansin* or someone a kinswoman or a neighbor recommends. Some women regularly consult the *mansin* during the first two weeks of the lunar New Year, then perform simple rituals, alone or with a *mansin*'s assistance, at the first full moon to protect vulnerable family members from anticipated misfortune during the year.

Illness attributed to hovering ghosts can be cleaned up with a simple exorcism, and some housewives exorcise family members without consulting a shaman. "Parents have to be half shamans *(pan mudang)* to raise up their children," my landlady told me when she deemed her daughter's cough and fever worthy of aspirin and an exorcism. My landlady brandished a kitchen knife at invisible baleful forces in the air above her daughter's pillow, then lured them into a gourd dipper filled with millet. She carried the dipper a safe distance from the house and cast the contents out. A *mansin*'s exorcism follows this same form but with more drama; the offending shades speak through the *mansin*'s lips and vent their grievances.

Persistent illness or a bundle of different but nearly simultaneous misfortunes implies that individual affliction is merely symptomatic of a deeper malaise within the house. In the *mansin*'s words, "The ancestors are hungry and the gods want to play." The family should sponsor an elaborate shaman ritual, a *kut,* to feast and entertain them. Financial loss, domestic quarrels, and illness can inspire a *kut.* This ritual revitalizes the entire house and household. The *mansin* purify the dwelling and invite the gods and ancestors inside. As the night progresses, gods and ancestors appear throughout the house and possess costumed shamans. They vent their grievances, provide divinations, receive tribute (gods) or sustenance (ancestors), and shower blessings on each member of the family. The *mansin* exorcise sick or unlucky family members and at the end of the *kut* cast lingering ghosts far away in the fields beyond the house gate.

Certain families have particularly powerful gods in their household pantheons—ancestors who held high positions, ancestresses who rigorously served the spirits, Mountain Gods and Seven Star Gods who gave the family sons. Capable of good or ill, these gods demand periodic homage, and neglect brings trouble. Women also deal with the ordinary dead, but under less friendly circumstances than when the men hold ancestor worship. Restless ancestors and ghosts and angry household gods bring affliction to the home—illness, financial loss, and domestic strife. The dead are dangerous simply because they are dead. They do not mingle well with the living and their touch brings illness or affliction. Even the compassionate touch of sympathetic ancestors brings illness to their children and grandchildren. More dangerous are familial dead who died with unfulfilled desires *(han):* grandparents who did not live to see their grandchildren, a first wife who was superseded by a second wife, a father who labored to provide for his family but died before he could taste his labor's fruit, young men and women who expired before they could marry and have children. If ancestor worship is a static show of respect, this darker side of the familial ideal makes family history a dynamic process. Longing souls mingle with the fate of the living until a shaman brings resolution.

These are the beliefs and activities that I have described in greater detail in *Shamans, Housewives, and Other Restless Spirits* (1985). In the process of synthesizing what I had learned, I came to appreciate that, while the general principles and possibilities of a religious system could be described in bold strokes, the religious life of each individual household was an emergent phenomenon,[3] a consequence of each family's spiritual history revealed and elaborated, time and again, in shaman divinations and *kut* and reaffirmed in women's memories. The existence of potent familial spirits usually implied stories about human encounters with spirits. In describing Korean women's religious lives, it seemed necessary to present the flavor of these personal and family histories, and to this end, I preserved the voices of several women who appeared and reappeared through several chapters under appropriate pseudonyms. Even so, the sweat and tears of their different lives were inevitably distilled to make an ethnographic text.[4] There is merit in retrieving one such life, in following an ethnography with a lengthy personal account that shows, among other things, how ethnographic constructs impinge upon the business of living and what one woman makes of them.

In her own story, Yongsu's Mother realizes the world of *Shamans,*

Housewives, and Other Restless Spirits as lived experience. She explains how and why she acquired her personalized set of potent spirits. Through these relationships and by her shaman destiny, she ascribes meaning and consequence to much that has befallen her. In meandering tales of her own construction, significant events come mingled with the happenstance of growing up, being disappointed in love, or raising her children, and assume the proportion that she ascribes to them. Cross-references to *Restless Spirits* reveal how Yongsu's Mother's voice was combined with those of other women to construct the original ethnographic text and set her experiences, at once extraordinary and thematic, amid a larger scheme.

Undoubtedly, I was the most consistently engaged audience that Yongsu's Mother had yet enjoyed and the spinning cassettes on my tape recorder vested her performance with a new aura of significance. Nevertheless, Korean women share their stories among themselves, and with her will to talk and knack for drama, Yongsu's Mother is especially good at recounting the amazing things that have happened to her.

"I looked up at my mother's face . . ."

She pauses, scans her audience, then continues in a whisper.

"My mother's face turned into a tiger."

"What in the world! . . ." the women gasp, nod, and cluck, huddled together in the warm room, a sympathetic chorus. In some sense these exchanges resemble a performance of Korean ballad opera *(p'ansori)* where the drummer's shouts of encouragement sustain the soloist, or, to use a more ordinary image, a one-sided Korean telephone conversation where the listener's periodic "*yea*s" mark the act of listening.

Yongsu's Mother's tales are punctuated by gestures and shifts in facial expression and colored by the changing pitch and cadence of her voice. Throughout the text, I have preserved in brackets a remembered grimace or roll of the eyes. This clumsy device makes a poor substitute for the immediacy of performance in an ethnographic film like Asch, Connor, and Asch's *Jero Tapakan: Stories from the Life of a Balinese Healer,* but even so, the reader is reminded that the tales had, when they were told, a more immediate audience.[5] Yongsu's Mother tells her life to edify her clients (as she would edify me) and to entertain her casual guests (as I was entertained). As a professional shaman she makes cautionary tales of the auspicious and inauspicious circumstances that have befallen her, her family, neighbors, and clients. Like all autobiography, Yongsu's Mother's tales are necessarily subjective, often exaggerated, and sometimes contradictory. They gain in ethnographic value precisely because she has told and retold them among clients and neighbors for a variety of personal and cultural reasons. With the force of personal history, she illustrates the power of a particular god, the baleful force of ancestral anger, or the danger of a ritual lapse. As a woman among women she seeks sympathy for the misfortunes and cruelties that she has experienced. As a professional shaman she engenders wonder at the evident hand of the gods in her destiny.

Over the years that I have known her, I have heard further repetitions and elaborations upon Yongsu's Mother's stories and gained some feeling for those events which she considers major turnings, the stories most often told and the incidents within stories that constitute their essential core, the part most polished, least variable, often underscored, and never omitted. I have also noticed that some tales are no longer told, perhaps because the circumstances that gave rise to memory or anger are no longer compelling. I have heard the essential core of nearly all of the tales presented here in both public and private renderings, in hours spent alone together and hours when village women crowded the hot floor of her inner room. Exceptions, tales for which I can recall no public telling, are her interrogation by the Red Army during the Korean War (in chapter 4), about which I raise some questions, and the contradictory story of an early love affair and birth of her illegitimate child (in chapter 6). Although I never heard her describe for others the circumstances surrounding the Willow Market Daughter's birth, she told me this sad story with all the rest and made no special point of it. Some of her neighbors did not seem to know the Willow Market Daughter's origins, but others did. Perhaps they, too, in some quiet and confidential moment, had been privy to the story. During my first field trip in 1977–1978, I failed to record a full text of the story of the little Buddha statue (in chapter 5), but I had heard bits and pieces and was able to request the tale in 1985.

Yongsu's Mother's story is precisely that, a story, not a "life history" or an "oral history" in the sense that these techniques are self-consciously employed by anthropologists and historians. I did not use a detailed interview schedule to dredge up specific biographical information or topical reminiscences from the murky vat of memory. Rather, a life story was thrust upon me. The circumstances of this encounter are described at length in chapter 2. Yongsu's Mother's tales were already more than twice told when first I heard them, and they would continue to be told long after I left the field.

The Anthropology of Life Stories

Social scientists have recognized the value of personal histories in rendering comprehensible the life and times of men and women in different cultural and historical circumstances. Because of their narrative form and intrinsic human interest, life histories are perhaps more easily consumed (and enjoyed) than other forms of ethnographic writing, while they have enduring scholarly value as near primary documents. Nevertheless, some anthropologists have always been uneasy with the business of recording a remembered and consequently subjective past (Boas 1943:334–335) and concerned that subjects be in some sense representative of the culture under study (Brandes 1982; Kluckhohn 1945; Langness 1965). The development of the life history method reflected the discipline's concern with verifiable and comparable data and with psychological anthropologists' interest in comparing personality development within and across cultures. One or several informants were to be carefully selected on the basis of predetermined criteria and asked to respond at length to topics elicited or prompted by the anthropologist (Langness 1965; Langness and Frank 1981; Watson and Watson-Franke 1985:1–29).

Harvey's *Six Korean Women: The Socialization of Shamans* (1979) is a skillful demonstration of the life history method. Since her subjects are, like Yongsu's Mother, female Korean shamans, I shall describe this valuable work in some detail to illustrate the manner in which Harvey's and my own are very different kinds of studies. Harvey addresses questions frequently asked in the study of shamanism and spirit possession: What is the relationship between women's ecstatic religious experiences and the mundane circumstances of women's lives? Does deprivation propel women and other oppressed groups into cathartic and redressive ritual activities (Lewis 1966, 1969)? Is this what motivates Korean women to become shamans? Apart from their common profession, Harvey's six informants defy easy generalization; they represent diverse class backgrounds, different degrees of exposure to traditional and modern influences, a variety of experiences in childhood, marriage, war, and migration, and an age span of several decades. As professional shamans, they range from the highly successful Pyŏngyang Mansin, who sends her children to study abroad, to Namsan Mansin, who tenuously sustains her family in a cramped rented room. Harvey interviewed each woman in the shaman's own home among her family and clients, slowly building rapport over several months. The interviews were structured only insofar as Harvey referred to a detailed questionnaire to guide informants toward discussions of childhood socialization, marital history, recruitment as a shaman, and subsequent performance of the shaman role. She relates that "the interactional process itself was generally very informal and spontaneous" (Harvey 1979:16). Harvey uses biographical material and observations of their family life to show how her informants carried a profound sense of injustice for hardships imposed on them as women and how, through the process of their possession and initiation, they were able to negotiate an authoritative role within their own families (Harvey 1980). These women attained something more than a vague catharsis; indeed, the professional status of the *mansin* is crucial to Harvey's analysis. She finds her informants to be extraordinarily intelligent, articulate, perceptive women who apply these talents to the shaman role and thereby make a good livelihood (Harvey 1979:235–240; Harvey 1980).

The life history method seems particularly well suited to the kind of problem that Harvey addresses, an issue profitably explored through the systematic collection of several shamans' life experiences. On the other hand, these several cases tell us very little about the women's own beliefs or how they, themselves, account for what has befallen them. It is a tribute to Harvey's skill as a writer, and not to the life history method per se, that we gain some sense of her informants as memorable personalities.

In recent years, several anthropologists have expressed dissatisfaction with the life history method, suggesting that there is something dishonest, or at least distorted, in the business of recording an informant's life history. They argue that, at worst, life material is forced into the ethnographer's a priori (and Western) notion of biography or determined by the ethnographer's categories of inquiry (Rosaldo 1976; Crapanzano 1977:22; Crapanzano 1980; Crapanzano 1984; Dwyer 1982; Little 1980). They remind us that the truth of an informant's life, like autobiographic truth, is shaped by the circumstances of the telling, and that memory and self-presentation are selective and sometimes self-contradictory processes (Frank 1979; Langness and Frank 1981). They have suggested that contradictory stories, and even outright fabrications, yield their own windows on the human soul (Crapanzano 1980, 1984). In the hands of these critics and innovators, the business of recording and interpreting life histories has become an increasingly self-conscious enterprise. We read more about the ethnographic encounter, both in the field and in retrospect, about the anthropologist's confrontation with the subjective truths of an informant's life, and about the anthropologist's struggle to interpret the informant's text through the informant's own premises. These concerns are commonly subsumed under the formidable headings of hermeneutics and phenomenology (Agar 1980; Watson 1976; Watson and Watson-Franke 1985:esp. 30–97). Interpretive challenges may be compounded when those who tell their lives are women in a culture that does not readily give them public voice, where they must use men's idiom to describe their lives (Young 1983), or where women articulate different models of self, person, and society than those we take for granted (Keesing 1985; Geiger 1986).

Only very recently, then, have we begun to ask why it is that people tell their lives, rather than why we should record them, and how it is that people fashion the tales that they tell. Yongsu's Mother's story can be instructive, reminding us that some among our informants are storytellers in their own lives and that the words they provide have not been given to us alone. I say "remind," for many anthropologists already knew this.

> Among the women I interviewed, Nisa stood out. She had an exceptional ability to tell a story in a way that was generous, vibrant, and moving. Her sensitivity and skill made her stories larger and more important than the details they comprised. (Shostak 1981:22)

> Manuel, by far the most fluent and dramatic storyteller in the family, needed relatively little editing. . . . The Manuel story, perhaps more than the others, however, loses a great deal in transcription and translation because he is a born actor with a great gift for nuance, timing, and intonation. A single question would often elicit an uninterrupted monologue of forty minutes. (Lewis 1963:xxi–xxii)

> "When Sylvie arrived, Mme. Jolan told me to stay around after dinner. I was surrounded by women and spent the evening telling them stories". . . . With genius, Tuhami was able to recreate this scene again and again

> in his later life. He has sat alone among women in traditional Moroccan households! His gift for storytelling and his clowning have enabled him to achieve this anomalous position in his own society, just as they had in the Jolan household. (Crapanzano 1980:60–61)

This business of performing, of making entertainments from the raw stuff of memory, is an enterprise distinct from and only serendipitously combined with the business of recording a life history. "I'll break open the story and tell you what is there," said Nisa to Marjorie Shostak. "Then, like the others that have fallen out onto the sand, I will finish with it and the wind will take it away" (Shostak 1981:39). In cold type Nisa's words are ironic, for Shostak has preserved them and made a text. Her words are also poignant, evoking the sense of mission that is implicit in much oral history and some ethno-biography. The subjects of ordinary lives are elusive; they are seldom encouraged to describe their own circumstances outside an intimate web of family reminiscence and community gossip and, the logic holds, they are less self-consciously articulate. "What's the use of knowing that?" my village informants would ask. Even if literate, they would probably not leave a record but for the fluke of a passing anthropologist or oral historian (Clifford 1980; Freeman and Krantz 1979).[6] Phillips speaks from the vantage point of a literate readership when he states, "the anthropologist's solicitation of the life history is usually the only reason for its existence, and his raw data comprise all the known information on the person being described" (Phillips' comment in Mandelbaum 1973:201). For our eyes, the life is in the text; Nisa, Manuel, and Tuhami "live" through the written words of Marjorie Shostak, Oscar Lewis, and Vincent Crapanzano. But in their own worlds, they live for as long as their stories are spoken, performed, and remembered. It is appropriate that contemporary writers have turned a critical eye to the process of constructing anthropological texts, to the manner of our own written intervention, and to the basis of our authority to speak of and for our subjects (Freeman and Krantz 1979; Myerhoff and Ruby 1982; Marcus and Cushman 1982). Meanwhile, some among our informants, and many who are not, continue to break open their stories and let them fall out onto the sand.

In presenting Yongsu's Mother's life, I would underscore this process of telling as it transpires in Yongsu's Mother's world. All of my recordings and observations are, of course, tainted. While Yongsu's

Mother told stories, I collected texts, frozen presentations that may not be at all representative of stories told in my absence. By observation, I know only that some of the same stories were told to many different audiences on various occasions over several years. I describe the manner in which my questions and my agendas influenced the flow of her narrative, and remark upon those themes that were probably inspired by my presence. I have rendered Yongsu's Mother's words into an English-speaking voice and made my own unabashed judgment on how she ought to sound. The process implies free rather than rigorously literal translations. I indicate where I have combined texts or have extensively pruned and rearranged them. In a few instances, I have included material not recorded and transcribed but rather reproduced from memory in my fieldnotes shortly after the conversation took place; these passages are also marked. The long, relatively uninterrupted flow of narrative in a given tale is a fair reproduction of what actually transpired and should convey both the rush of Yongsu's Mother's words and the force of her personality.

Yongsu's Mother presents herself as a well-intentioned, compassionate, clever woman, often wronged, but never crushed, never ground down to total defeat. Even so, something of her combativeness and extreme sensitivity show through, and these traits serve her for both good and ill. Although she attributes much that has befallen her to destiny or divine will, this makes her no less a fighter. She strikes a posture reminiscent of so many Korean women at a *kut* who, when they confront their gods in the person of a possessed shaman, banter, wheedle, tease, argue, and contend.[7] As a newly initiated shaman, she listens for guidance from her voices, but could one imagine Joan of Arc arguing, as Yongsu's Mother does (in chapter 6), that her voices have imposed upon her a task that is both illogical and excessive?

Women's Lives and Shamans' Stories

Despite the best efforts of anthropologists, sociologists, and social historians, we expect to know more about privileged lives than impoverished ones, more about men than women, and least of all about illiterate or partially educated women. Not only are women less often literate (Geiger 1986:335), they may impose their own silence for lack of confidence and self-esteem (Chamberlain [1975] 1983:11), perceptions sometimes reinforced by those who would record their lives (Watson and Watson-Franke 1985:163). We would thus expect to have very little information on the lives of ordinary Korean women, and this is indeed the case (Clark 1986; Kendall and Peterson 1983). The one known example of a premodern but still far from ordinary Korean woman's autobiography is remarkable insofar as the very necessity of making a written record becomes further evidence of the author's extraordinarily bitter circumstances (Haboush 1986). It is therefore surprising that accounts of female shamans' lives abound. With the exception of Harvey's *Six Korean Women* (1979) and single portraits by Ch'oe (1981) and Wilson (1983), however, most of these treatments seem to be extremely cursory; they do not give us the women's own words and rarely convey a sense of fully realized personalities living their lives in their times.

The anthropologists, folklorists, psychologists, and religious historians who have recorded Korean shamans' lives share the interests of an international community of scholars engaged in research on shamanism, from its inception a study in case studies.[8] The sheer volume of their publications, however, might also suggest something of the role of autobiography in the *mansin*'s own life and practice. Why, after all, are Korean shamans such generally accommodating informants? Why should Yongsu's Mother volunteer to tell me her life? Why should Suwŏn Mansin even think to solicit Harvey's attention (1979:174–176)? A partial answer may be found in Harvey's characterization of her *mansin* informants as intelligent, articulate, perceptive women, vested with a strong sense of their own worth (Harvey 1979:235–240). These are the attributes of good storytellers, these are not the attributes of muted women in a culture that denies them voice. This is not what we would expect of Confucian Korea, given the pervasive stereotype of humble wives and long-suffering mothers. Yongsu's Mother is very much the central character of her own narration, confounding the common observation that women, East and West, submerge their autobiographical identities in the lives of others (Bertaux-Wiame 1981:260; Lebra 1984:294–295; cf. Watson and Watson-Franke 1985:163–170). Is Yongsu's Mother's assertiveness the consequence of a particular fate that made her assume formidable responsibilities at an early age? More generally, are Korean shamans unusual Korean women, as Harvey suggests (1979, 1980), or are their lives only slight exaggerations upon more general patterns of Korean feminine behavior, as I have implied (Kendall 1985)? An adequate answer awaits the recorded lives of ordinary Korean women. As we begin to hear their voices every so often in ethnographies, we find intimations of much more worth our listening.[9]

TWO

A Tale of Deceit and a Tale of Kam'ak Mountain

The most nerve-wracking days come early in fieldwork. My assistant and I went from door to door administering a routine survey questionnaire. How many people live in this house? What are their ages? We asked about childbirth, miscarriages, and abortions; about spirit possession, exorcisms, and divinations. We took great pains to explain the purpose of my study, but our carefully rehearsed and excessively polite introductions did not lull my own discomfort at intruding upon the lives of busy country women, blundering upon better ways to ask key questions and struggling to make sense of the things that we were told.

In the lingering April dusk, we went to Yongsu's Mother's house because we needed a lift, and this would be an easy interview. I had already spent more than a month in the shaman's company at divination sessions and shaman rituals; she knew that my work included a constant barrage of questions, and I knew that Yongsu's Mother loved to talk. She fielded our queries with an air of amusement, prompting my assistant to giggling self-parody.

"Do you practice birth control?"

"Am I a chicken? Can I lay eggs without a mate?"

And so we continued. Her stepson, aged nineteen, now there was a worry! He had given up studying so she bought him a cow to raise, but then his elder sister (that bitch) lured him away to work for her instead. Yongsu's Mother, stuck with the cow, sold it at a loss. She was still smarting from this most recent evidence of her stepchildren's ingratitude. Her recollections of her own family tapped an older betrayal. Her father had died when he was shot by an invisible supernatural arrow *(kunung sal)* at a funeral feast.[1] She didn't miss him at all, though, or even want to think about him, because he had taken a concubine and given his own children grief.

The anthropologist and her assistant were an appreciative audience, a sympathetic audience, and the shaman would give us more than the routine answers our tedious questions solicited. She told us about the little sister who had died of smallpox. The family held a *kut* for the smallpox spirit *(mama kut),* and the shamans jumped up and down on the porch with such enthusiasm that the floorboards caved in. When the smallpox spirit visits the house, nails should not be driven into wood, but her father ignored the prohibition and repaired the broken porch. The sick child went blind. They searched for the nails, found one, pulled it out, washed it, and the little girl regained sight in one eye. Still, she remained sickly and soon died, cradled in her elder sister's arms. Yongsu's Mother claims not to have realized that her little sister, suddenly quiet in her embrace, was dead. Her mother sent her to fetch their father from his concubine's house. He purchased a small coffin, and that evening people came to take it away.

Yongsu's Mother keeps the little girl's spirit with the gods and ancestors in her shrine. When she performs *kut* to feast and entertain her own gods, she ties a child's brightly colored skirt and jacket to the belt of the costume she wears to summon the Special Messenger (Pyŏlsang), the smallpox spirit. Her dead sister comes to the *kut* in the god's entourage; I would meet her at a *kut* in Yongsu's Mother's shrine later that spring. Speaking through the lips of a possessed *mansin,* she would announce herself as a Princess (Hogu) and claim that she had come to play.[2]

From the loose threads of the survey questions, Yongsu's Mother began to spin bits of tales, constrained and abbreviated by the structure of our interview and the list of questions yet to be posed. When we asked about marriage, the dam burst and the words poured out, rising and falling until the tale was told.

My children's father died of drink, crude vodka *(soju).* When he carried me off, he lied. He lied about his age. He had three children but he claimed that he only had two. He lied about their ages, too. I told my sister, "He looks older than he says." I wanted her to have him investigated, to see if he was telling us the truth, but she just said, "The matchmaker will take care of everything."[3] I felt numb inside. I went out to the chimney flue behind the house and I cried and cried. I thought, "Does my sister hate me so much that she wants to make me suffer? Does it take so much rice to feed me?"

The beginning was disjointed; she had sliced obliquely into an already polished narrative. Her usual audience of village women and clients would have heard it all before, as I would hear it again.

I'd moved down to the country because my mother wanted to settle near my sister in Willow Market. I was born in Seoul and raised in Seoul, and I wanted to live in Seoul. I'd worked for the printing company for ten years or more, so if I went back to Seoul, there would be friends who could help me get by. It was the tenth month, and I thought that if I could just get through the winter down here, I'd go back up to Seoul. But my sister was determined to marry me off.

It was market day, I can never forget it. We'd been boiling beans to make soy sauce. I was dressed up in a yellow jacket and a pink skirt, silky stuff, the best you could get back then. I had on my best Korean dress and fresh white stockings. I thought I'd go down and see what the Willow Market was like, and I was on my way out of the gate when a man and a woman arrived. The man asked me, "Is your elder sister home?" I just bawled back, "Sister, someone's here!" She came bustling out to greet them and took them straight to our mother's room. I told Mom I was going out, but she sent me to stoke the fire under the beans.

I kept tossing twigs into the flames while my sister, behind the paper door, kept saying, "Yes, yes, yes." I stuck my head in and asked, "What's going on?" She told me to get some noodle soup from the Chinese restaurant. I asked, "What about me?" "You can do as you like." So I went and ordered their noodle soup, and when the restaurant boy delivered it, I set it on a tray with some kimchee and shouted in, "Here's the noodles!" My sister told me to come in and sit down. I just plopped the tray down and trudged back outside. I didn't think anything of it, didn't realize they'd come to look me over *(sŏn poda)*. I thought that they had come to see my sister and I'd just brought them some noodles for lunch. The man sat by the desk with a handkerchief on his lap and he looked very old. I remembered that afterward. I'd just walked in and out when I brought the noodles.

My sister called for me to take away the tray, so I went back in. That guy hadn't eaten more than three mouthfuls. I took his noodles out to the kitchen to save for later. When my mother came out, I asked her if I could go to the market. She said, "What's all this about going to the market? Where's the money?" I told her I had money, and she asked me where I'd kept it hidden. There wasn't anything to buy out in the country anyway. I just wanted to have a look around.

The man was ready to leave, and everyone stood around saying their good-byes. I stayed in the kitchen, but as soon as the man left, the match-maker came looking for me. She said she wanted to have a talk. I told her I was going to the market. She said, "You come right over here and tell me what you think of that guy."

"What do you mean?"

"He's looked you over and you please him. Just say the word and it's settled."

I was flabbergasted. "What nonsense is this? Who says I want to get married? Anyway, I wouldn't marry an old guy like that. Don't even say such things!"

The matchmaker went right back into my sister's room. I wasn't in the mood for the market anymore. I waited for the matchmaker to come out and she started in again, "Tell me what you thought of that guy, just say the word. He's all right, isn't he?"

I howled that I couldn't go through with it. I told them, "Do you think I can't find a husband anywhere? Do you think I have to settle for an old guy like that? I'm going back to Seoul."

Then my sister raised a fuss. "You're so stubborn! With your wretched bad fate, you should marry an older man, someone who's already been married once.[4] I'm your sister. Do you think I'd arrange something that was bad for you?"

When she said that, I was so furious I couldn't hold it in, I ran to the chimney behind the house and sobbed. "She brought us down here because she was lonely. She's made us sell our house. Why is she doing this to me? When the right time comes, I'll gladly get married. Why do they have to marry me off to an old guy?" I raged and cried, and raged some more.

My mother found me and asked why I was crying, but she's never been able to stand up to my sister. She couldn't order me to marry, but she couldn't prevent the marriage either. My sister was out in front of the house, banging on the wooden porch with her fist and shouting, "They're killing me, they're killing me! My brothers and sisters will be the death of me!"

I thought it over. I thought, "Do you hate me so much that you could just hand me over to anyone who passes by?" In the end I capitulated, "I don't know how it'll turn out, but if things go badly, I'll never think of you as my sister again. You're just doing this because you don't want to feed me." That was what I thought to myself. Out loud I said, "Do what you will. Have it your way." She thought I had agreed.

My sister said, "This isn't an auspicious year for her wedding, so we'll wait until the twelfth month."[5]

"If it isn't a good year for a wedding, why are you in such a rush to get rid of me?"

"Go to Seoul, and who'll feed you? Typhoid take you!"

"You're my elder sister and you act as though you were doing right by me, but we'll just see what happens."

That man came back three days later. This time I was so mad I didn't even want to look at him. They called for me but I went to the outhouse instead, pulled the door softly shut, and sat quietly inside. After a while, he left.

He came to the house often, but I just pretended not to see him. If he came in this way, I went out that way. He'd go into my mother's room and then they would all sit around talking.

We passed into the twelfth month, the empty time that we don't consider part of the old year. About five days before the wedding, the man gave my sister some money for my permanent and bride's makeup. I took the money and threw it on the ground. "What does this have to do with anything? Does he think I haven't gotten married because I can't afford to permanent my hair?" My sister tried to coax me, but this threw me into a deeper rage. "If I'm set against him, why are you all so anxious to throw me out like this? If our ages were similar it would be all right, but he's old. If you're so keen on this marriage, why not go and investigate him? Do you expect me to marry someone who lives so far away on just the strength of the matchmaker's words?"

"The matchmaker knows the whole story. How come you're suspicious like a Chinaman?"

I left Willow Market with him and cried all the way on the bus. My eyes were swollen. It must have been embarrassing for him. [A mischievous smirk flashes across her lips and disappears.]

We got to the Imjin River. That was as far as the bus would go. We needed passes to board the boat, but I said I didn't have one. We had a huge fight right there on the dock. Here I was, all done up in a Korean dress made of silk from Hong Kong, and the angrier I got, the more I wanted to throw myself into the river. By the time my husband had cleared things with the guards and dragged me away to the boat my feet were frozen stiff. On the other side there was another checkpoint. The guard asked me, "Auntie, do you have a citizen's identification card?" This time I just slipped out my Seoul registration card, showed the guard, and walked on through. [She pantomimes her gesture of feigned nonchalance.]

As we reached the far side of the river, someone rode up on a bicycle, parked it on the sand, and pulled in the boat. I thought it was just another passenger going to cross the river, but when I looked I saw that he resembled my husband. I'd heard that he had six brothers so I just assumed that this was one of them, but when I asked my husband, he denied it, said it was a distant relation. Even on the way to his home he lied to me.

We walked and walked. My feet swelled up like balloons. I wasn't used to walking. Finally, we came to the village. A girl emerged from one of the houses and threw out a basin of dishwater. She gave me the strangest look. In some odd way she seemed to resemble my husband. She was standing in front of a straw-roofed house, a tumble-down house, it was falling apart at the seams. It looked just like Ch'un Hyang's house.[6] I hoped with all my might that we would not turn into that house. I followed behind my husband with my eyes cast down to the backs of his shoes. His feet turned into that very gateway. Could he just be stopping by? No such luck. As soon as we were inside the gate, I heard, "Daddy's home, Daddy's home!" Despair!

I stood there in the gateway, stunned. I heard them ask me, over and over again, to come in. There was a three-year-old boy, a little frog baby looking mischievous, and a nine-year-old daughter, the one who works in Seoul now. There was a twenty-one-year-old daughter; I was barely five years older than her. I thought she was my husband's niece. I thought that she had just come over to help with the housework.

They kept asking me to come inside, so I went in and looked things over. It was laughable; the house was bare. The cupboard held one battered little dish for shrimp sauce. Oh, I was disappointed! I just stood there in the empty kitchen until my husband took me by the hand and led me to the inner room. It was a sorry show there too, only a wooden chest and some quilts piled up. I cursed my fucking sister! Why did I deserve this? That bitch! I had told her to check everything before she married me off. I cried and cried. I couldn't stop. My husband said, "What's done is done. You won't get anywhere by crying about it." But I was fuming. If my sister had lived nearby, I'd have gone right over and grabbed her. I'd have dragged her there and said, "Feast your eyes on this!" But I didn't know the way back; I had never been in this village before.

The older girl brought in a tray of food. All of the relatives came over.

The elder brothers' wives and the elder cousins' wives served the food—rice, toasted seaweed, and kimchee.[7] Since it was the twelfth month, we ate winter kimchee. They kept asking me to eat and I kept saying that I didn't want any. They asked and I refused, again and again. That person, my husband, couldn't eat either. When the elder brother's wife *(sŏng)* came in and begged me to eat, I had a few mouthfuls just to make them happy.

Then I had to bow to them all.[8] The room was full of people; they swarmed around like maggots. I had no idea who they were. There were relatives to the third degree *(sam ch'on)* and relatives to the fourth degree *(sa ch'on)*. I was dropping down to the floor and bobbing up all night. Finally, the third brother's wife said, "She's had a long journey. She must be tired. Those who haven't received her bows can come back tomorrow." My husband told them that my feet were swollen.

After everyone left [now, in the telling, she rolls her eyes to the ceiling], that man, my husband, went outside too. The brothers' wives were fixing a late night snack. The girl came into the room to get something. She looked at my hand and said, "What a lovely hand!" She asked how old I was. My husband had told me to say that I was thirty-six but I told the truth, "I'm twenty-six."

The girl started, "Twenty-six?"

The brother's wife said, "Your skin is still soft like a baby's. With such a lovely face and hands, how can you do a country woman's work?" They said, "Your ages are too far apart." They chattered on about how young I was and how old he was while I just sat there. The girl came back into the room. I asked, "How old are you?"

She said, "One."

I said, "You mean twenty-one?"

She nodded.

The brother's wife explained, "The little father (junior uncle) is forty-one." Now it dawned on me that this girl was my husband's daughter. I thought, "It will be difficult enough to raise my own children, but how am I ever going to raise these?"

It was already one o'clock in the morning. They rolled out the quilts and told me to rest. My husband came in and sent them all home so I could sleep. He went out to see them off and came back. I couldn't even cry. I just sat there without a word. He came over and tried to take off my jacket. When he reached for the ribbon, I slapped his hand away.[9] I said, "You should have told me the truth. You should have told me that you're forty-one years old and have a twenty-one-year-old daughter. After lying like this, how dare you put your hand to my body!"

Now he was angry, "Who told you that?" But then he said, "Don't worry about my daughter. I'll just marry her off. If I said I had so many daughters, they wouldn't have given you to me. I lied about that, but I really am thirty-seven years old."

I said, "All right, tomorrow we'll go to the district office and just see how you're registered. I've come all this way. If you turn out to be thirty-seven, I'll stay, but if that's not so, I'm leaving."

I didn't sleep. I held my ground all night. Whenever he reached out to touch me, I slapped his hand away. What could he do? He sat there smoking. He offered to help me take off my padded socks because my feet were sore. I said, "If my feet hurt, that's my business. You leave me alone."

In the morning, the older daughter fixed breakfast and the elder brother's wife came over to help. I stayed in the inner room. When the nine-year-old girl brought water for me to wash my face she said, "How can this person be my mother?" My husband hit her. He scolded her in a loud voice that all the relatives could hear. It did not bode well for a daughter to be disrespectful to her new stepmother.

They brought in the breakfast tray and again I said that I wasn't going to eat. I hadn't eaten anything for so long that my eyes were turning back inside my head. My husband went out and spoke to his brother's wife. She came in and coaxed, "Since you're here, you might as well eat something. Here, let's eat together." I could have eaten everything on that tray, but I just had a couple of spoonfuls. When she took out the tray, I heard my husband ask how I was. I sat in the room all day without saying a word. He fretted and paced back and forth, back and forth. I can still hear the sound of his feet. He was worried that I might run away. He was worried that I didn't eat. He paced back and forth, and three days went by.[10]

On the third day, they usually send the bride back to her relatives for a visit. I got up early and swept the wooden porch. I polished the smooth boards to a shine. My husband gave me some money to go and have my hair curled, and pointed the direction because I didn't know the way. I had my hair curled and came back, but then he wouldn't let me go home. He said he would take me there by and by, but he was afraid that I might run away.

Hours had passed. We were summoned to a late dinner while she hastened to cook up the evening rice for herself and Yongsu. We returned again in the evening and listened into the night. Later, when we had translated all that we had heard and recorded, we knew that we were hooked, avid to hear more. Not only did Yongsu's Mother provide a rich ethnographic narrative, she was a skilled storyteller, rendering her images with delicious turns of phrase. Her feet swelled up like balloons. She kept stoking the fire while her sister kept saying, "Yes, yes, yes." She modestly lowered her gaze to the backs of her husband's feet and saw them turn into the doorway of the hovel that would be her new home. She remembered details: the handkerchief on her future husband's lap, the pot of boiling beans, the half-eaten bowl of noodles, the basin of water in her stepdaughter's hands.

I toyed with the idea of recording a full biography, but was soon preoccupied by my research on shaman rituals. My assistant, who had relished the task of translating Yongsu's Mother's vivid language, left the field when she landed a promising job in Seoul. As I have explained, it was Yongsu's Mother who took the initiative, by announcing that she would tell me the full story of her life. She had already mapped out the narrative: "the story of my childhood and of my father's taking a concubine, the story of my capture and escape during the war and my meeting with the Mountain God, the story of my lover and the birth of my daughter, the story of my marriage, and the story of my becoming a *mansin.*" She told me that when I knew it all my tears would flow. The recurrent themes of her life had already been sounded in the initial interview: betrayal by kin, disappointment in human relationships, the bother and ingratitude of stepchildren, and the power of gods and ancestors to alter human destiny for good or ill. The story of her wedding journey, recounted above, appears again as she told it in chronological sequence (see chapter 6). A comparison of the two renderings suggests that by the time I first heard it, her tale had already become the polished product of many recitations in the company of other women.

Does art imply artifice? Does artifice detract from the value of an autobiographical text? I suspect that Yongsu's Mother often exaggerates, both to vindicate herself and also to heighten the drama of her performance. Hers is a melodramatic account, told among people who appreciate the purgative value of a good cry. This is not to say that she consciously deceives her audience, but rather that she plays her material for all it's worth. When she told us the story of her marriage, I saw, with the telling, a young girl. "I'm going to the market." With a soft and childish voice she recreated the innocent maiden of a fairy tale, oblivious to the machinations of a greedy sister who was sealing her fate behind closed doors. The fairy tale became a comic opera when she gracelessly delivered the noodles to her would-be suitor. But how naive could she have been? Not only was she twenty-six years old when she married the widower, she had already given birth to an illegitimate child. By the bitter standards of her own society, the bride was past marrying age and damaged goods besides. The scheming sister might rather have tried to make the best of her younger sibling's limited options.

The graceless delivery of the noodles is also suspicious. Why was the prospective bride dressed up in her best yellow jacket and pink skirt on the day they boiled beans to make soy sauce? In the early 1960s, when these events took place, it was not unusual for a representative of the groom's family to pose as a casual guest and thereby covertly examine the bride's deportment, grace, and appearance. The maiden, carefully dressed and combed but seemingly uncoached, would demurely present a tray of food or a bowl of water to the visitor. Yongsu's Mother, decked out in her finery, must have suspected that something was afoot. Was her artless behavior a counterploy, an attempt to capitalize upon her assumed innocence? Could the spoiled market trip have been a thwarted strategy of escape?

Although the narrative dissolves into empty threats and a capitulatory trip to the beauty parlor, Yongsu's Mother had been true to her own strong spirit. She went not silent to her husband's house, but protesting every inch of the way. Once there, however, she recognized her lack of alternatives, cut her losses, made a life, and spun out her anger in a tale. Her art was to make old disappointment a good story.

In the spring of 1977 her marriage and its consequences were a sore topic. She was vexed with her ungrateful stepchildren and with the loneliness and insecurity of her widowhood. Village gossips told me that her flowering friendship with a local widower had been crushed by his fractious daughter-in-law. Normally active and vivacious, now Yongsu's Mother sat at home and brooded or poured out her thoughts to the anthropologist, her *mansin* colleagues, and the village women. Telling her life, she probed the past, seizing reasons for her present misery. The villains in the tale of her marriage were her imprudent elder sister, whom she still considered a cheapskate, and the deceitful groom. The man had lied about his age, his wherewithal, and his children. Worst of all, after leading her into the trap of hardship, he had died.

Gloominess and a brief illness in the early spring suggested that her personal spirits, the gods and ancestors of her shrine, were impatient for tribute. As the days grew longer, Yongsu's Mother began to plan her flower-greeting *kut,* an annual ritual to feast and entertain her own gods, ancestors, and clients.[11] Well done, the *kut* would change her luck. Before the *kut,* she would make a pilgrimage up Kam'ak Mountain and invoke the powerful gods of the place, calling them down from the mountain to her shrine.[12] She would prepare herself with a three-day fast from meat and fish, bathe in pure, cold water, and leave the village in silence, neither giving nor returning greetings. On the mountain, she would boil clean rice and make her offerings to the Water Grandmother (Mulsin Halmŏni) of the well and the Mountain God (Sansin) on the summit, and then she would return in silence. If she should see a snake or dead frog or hear of a recent death in the village, she would have to abandon her pilgrimage. I was invited to accompany Yongsu's Mother and two other *mansin,* to leave the village at dawn, travel by bus and taxi to the foot of Kam'ak Mountain, and climb to the summit.

Kam'ak Mountain is near the country village that Yongsu's Mother had entered more than a decade before as a reluctant bride. When the wives of her husband's family, the Yuns, had honored the God of Kam'ak Mountain, their families had flourished. Marriage links Yongsu's Mother to Kam'ak Mountain, but she began her married life ignorant of the powerful Mountain God. The Yun wives of her generation had ignored the custom and suffered the consequences.

My husband's father had two wives. The first wife had a son, but she died. The second wife wore a beaded crown as a bride because she was a maiden. This was my husband's mother. She had five sons and two daughters, and she raised all those children. She sent her daughters to their husbands' homes and saw all of her sons take wives before she died.

But look at them now! The first son had three daughters, but whenever sons were born, they barely lived past the first year. In that household they simply could not raise a son. The second brother died with no children at all. The third brother has two sons and the fourth is childless. I have my two boys and the sixth brother has one son. Even if you give a son to each sonless brother's house, it doesn't add up to even one son for each family. You see why they say, "To raise up your children, use Kam'ak Mountain."

The eldest brother's house, the big house *(k'ŭnjip)*, doesn't use the mountain, nor does the second house. The big house believes in Jesus. They found an adopted son-in-law for the daughter, but that couple is Christian; they use the father's property but they don't even give him ancestor rites *(chesa)*. The uncles made a fuss about it, "If you're going to live off of your father's property, you should honor him. We'll adopt an heir who'll give your father his due, and then you can just get out." But the uncles who had the authority to say things like that are all dead now. The youngest brother? He believes in Jesus too. Originally he didn't, but his wife's family is Christian so he started believing in Jesus after his marriage. This last brother's wife died before she had reached her full sixty years.

No one in our generation used the mountain, not the third house, not the fourth house, and we didn't either. My husband was opposed to shaman rituals and that sort of thing, so how would I know to use the mountain? I was young, I didn't understand. My sisters-in-law are the ones who should have showed me what to do, but they lacked respect for the mountain. How was I to know?

The Yun family has fallen apart, and all because of Kam'ak Mountain. They're all widows and widowers now. The big house ended without sons and the second house died out too. We're the fifth house and look at us. I'm a widow living alone. The sixth brother is the only one of the uncles left, but his wife is dead and that uncle has his troubles. He went to Seoul and brought back a widow. Now there are problems because the kids aren't her children. [This is an unacknowledged parallel to her own marriage.]

People should be born, marry, and grow old, reach their sixty-first and seventy-first years. It's no good when they die young. Now my sons are growing up without a father. We call the youngest uncle "Little Father" (Chagŭn Abŏji) and he should be like their father. My sons (Yongsu and the stepson) adored his first wife; they used to call after her, "Little Mother, Little Mother," but there's no affection between them and the new little mother. We don't visit back and forth anymore.

The old grandmother, my mother-in-law, was an ignorant country woman, but she used the mountain and things worked out for her. Her children forgot the mountain, and everything went wrong. I'm going to use Kam'ak Mountain and pray that my sons will turn out well. I'm the only one from my husband's family who goes there now. I told the new little mother,

"Our mother-in-law used Kam'ak Mountain, so now we ought to do it," but she just said, "How could I do something like that?" It's her affair whether she goes or not. Who am I to say do this and do that? Before I became a *mansin* I didn't appreciate these things. I was young when I married and didn't know what I know now. If I had used the mountain, maybe my husband would still be alive. He drank himself to death on rotgut vodka, and he told me a pack of lies.

Misfortunes have a complex causality and Yongsu's Mother will offer several reasons for her widowhood. On this occasion, her anger at her drunken and deceitful spouse is mingled with her respect for the powerful Mountain God who might have spared him. The god is a link to the time of her marriage, a part of the Yun family's supernatural heritage that she now channels to her own household. Yongsu's Mother spoke of the mountain to educate the anthropologist, bı while she gave me an edifying example of beliefs and practices assc ciated with the Mountain God, the Yun family's demise was a persona parable. The story of the mountain became an account of her hus band's kin. Then, again, she tapped the well of pain and anger, th memory of her brief marriage.

THREE

Born in an Unlucky Hour

In May men and women labored in the mud and wet of the paddy fields, bending in unison to set down row after row of jade green rice shoots. The villagers' busy season began with the warmer weather, and the *mansin*'s came to an end. In the early spring, Yongsu's Mother had gone hither and thither to *kut,* invoking and propitiating the angry gods and restless ancestors that had loomed ominously in her clients' New Year's divinations. When the flowers began to bloom on village hillsides, the *mansin* held flower-greeting *kut (kkonmaji kut)* to feast and entertain all of their own gods and clients, bustling back and forth between the shrines to assist each other. All that was over now. A few clients visited the shrine, prompted by illness or domestic problems. A few *kut* were held, mostly in the market town, and perspiration rolled down the faces of the costumed, dancing *mansin.*

Yongsu's Mother spent more time at home, tending her own vegetable garden, divining for an occasional client, and making elaborate preparations for the ritual offerings that would mark her husband's death anniversary. The anthropologist was also idle. Reluctant to continue my survey when so many village households were at work in the paddy or vegetable plots, I spent more time at Yongsu's Mother's house. In between my other queries, she began to narrate the story of her life, summarized thus grimly in that initial interview: "I was born at seven in the morning on the eighth day of the third lunar month. I should have been born in the evening, and so my fate is wretched *(p'alchaga sanapta).* They told me I should marry late, but even that didn't help because my husband died anyway." A bad marriage had failed to circumvent an inauspicious horoscope. The words sound fatalistic, but in Yongsu's Mother's mouth they bespeak vexation, not resignation. From childhood, and against formidable odds, she has always been a scrapper.

Before she was anyone's mother, she was a girl called Changmi, a name no longer used in direct address but preserved on official documents and on my survey form. This is her recollection of Changmi's life. She begins at the beginning.

When I was a baby our family was poor, so poor that my mother went out peddling. My mother says that I cried too much; she couldn't leave me behind. Every day she took me on her back and carried me around with her. That was why her feet used to swell up and throb and throb. When I had grown just a bit, my mother had another baby, my younger brother. My mother told me, "Come and take a look!" but when I saw my baby brother, I burst into tears. I didn't like him at all. Oh how I cried!

Where was your elder sister?

My elder sister? She was gone.

But she was not gone so much as she was irrelevant to this tale. She married at age eighteen, just in time to escape the worst hardships of Changmi's youth.

My sister was the eldest child, then my older brother, then me, then my younger brother, a sister, then another sister, and then my youngest brother. That's how it was.

We grew, my little brother and I, and when I was five or six years old, we caught the measles. My mother says that she didn't fret too much about my measles since I was just a girl. My brother was a boy and she was only anxious about him; she fretted about my younger brother but not about me. My mother says that even though I had the measles, I would run outside to play. I'd go out and then come back in and then go back outside again. My mother kept my little brother inside; if he should so much as be caught in a draft, it would be all over and he'd die. Both of us were sick, but she put her son on the warm part of the heated floor and put me on the cold part.[1] She just set me there to die, but she carefully nursed my little brother.

Well then, my brother gave a rattling gasp and died. As for me, the measles went pop, pop and went away. Wasn't that a surprise? How could it be that the son she had fretted over had died and the daughter that she had left for dead had lived? Now that the illness had passed, my mother went out peddling again.

She had heard this story from her mother and retold it with a mingling of pride and irony at her own survival. Perhaps the little girl had had only a light case of measles and the boy had been far more seriously ill. Perhaps the mother needed to reassure herself, against possible recriminations, that she had exerted every possible effort to save her male issue. I have sometimes winced at Korean parents' seemingly callous statements, made within earshot of or even addressed to their children (Kendall n.d.a; Janelli and Janelli 1982:36). "We wanted a boy, but this wretch of a girl here was born instead." "This daughter is pretty, but this one has no looks at all." The youngest sister in my fictive family announced to me, with the seeming unconcern of a jolly five-year-old, that she had been returned to the family wrapped in a blanket after her impoverished parents had tried to sell her. Her mother took up the story, relating how the prospective American father had rejected the baby as looking too Asian, "with her tiny little dark eyes; he didn't like that." I noticed then, and on other occasions, that these blunt remarks were usually tinged with a gentle humor at life's irrevocable twists of circumstance, and sometimes delivered while hugging the ill-favored child.

I have often wondered how children bear such declarations, frequently repeated during their growing up. I doubt that they hear only the words and miss the affection that so often accompanies them. Nevertheless, there is an unmistakable sense of injustice in Yongsu's Mother's story. As a *mansin,* she is thoroughly familiar with the *Tale of Princess Pari (Pari Kongju),* an epic ballad recited during the *kut* for the dead (Kendall 1985:154, 196n.8; Kim 1966). As the unwanted seventh daughter of a sonless king and queen, Princess Pari is cast out to die. Rescued and coached in magic, Princess Pari braves the perils of the netherworld to find the magic herb that will restore her stricken parents. When Yongsu's Mother told me a simplified version of Princess Pari's story, she told the tale with feeling. Implicit in the tale of Princess Pari is the message that unwanted daughters have unacknowledged powers and a stubborn will to survive and be vindicated. A parallel theme runs through Yongsu's Mother's own tale, and like Princess Pari, Changmi would travel to the brink of hell and back. But that was in the future.

It was around the time of the liberation. The Japanese were still here when I started school. I was nine years old when they left. Our family was very poor then, so my mother brewed wine and sold it to a wine house.

Was your father still at home?

He certainly was. He sold vegetables in the market, buying them wholesale and then retailing them. In the fall, when the apples, pears, and soft persimmons came in, he'd buy them up and resell them. But my father was such a philanderer! He liked nothing more than wine, *kisaeng*,[2] and raising a racket. He ought to have brought money home, but every day he went to the wine house or the brothel instead. What could my mother do? She had to make a living so we could get by. She had to have some sort of business. My mother would brew wine in a great, huge pot and sell it to the wine house. She'd make the soup we drink as a tonic for hangovers *(haejang kuk)*, and she'd sell that too.

When I was nine years old, my brother went to X—— Elementary School and I went to Y—— Elementary School. Because he was a son, he was supposed to study, but since I was a girl, my father told me to stop. I liked school, so I went anyway. Things went on like this until I was ten years old. I took the second-year examination and passed it. My brother made scores of 50, 60, and 40, while I made scores of 85, 90, and 100. We stood in front of our father and he said, "Let me see your test scores." I handed him my paper, but my brother refused since he had received low scores. I teased him, "Elder Brother, hand your test scores over, hand them over," until he gave them up.

My father compared our scores and said, "Bitch! I didn't want the girl to study, but she's done well. Why can't this stupid boy learn anything?" He really raised a commotion. We stood there cowering. Then he told me, "If you so much as set foot in school, I'll beat you."

My mother had been peddling soup so she had a little money that she gave me on the sly. She gave me money for the monthly tuition and told me to buy pens and notebooks. Since I was a good student, my mother intended to send me to school. I asked my father to buy me some shoes, but he wouldn't, so I went to school in my bare feet. My bare feet! I'm telling you that I ran away to school in my bare feet. My mother did the best she could and bought me some *geta* made out of bits of wood. If I wore those things all the way to school, the strings would snap. I carried them with my book bag all the way to school. Even at home, if I so much as put them on to step outside, the strings would break again. I was exasperated with those shoes. I went around in my bare feet.

Another day, she took up the story and told me again about sneaking off to school, running away in her bare feet with her book bag and the troublesome *geta* in her hands. She added these details.

When I was in primary school, there wasn't any rice. I went to school hungry. I thought only of my empty stomach and wasn't able to concentrate. My father was a terror. He'd say that a girl shouldn't study and would chase after me, waving a stick. But I ran away and escaped. When he had gone, when he was already asleep, I snuck inside and went to sleep myself . . . I ran off to school on the sly. Even if I was so hungry I could die, I couldn't go home if my father was there. I was too frightened. I'd go home, but then I would hide under the porch. One day I passed my father's shop on my way back from school.

"Where've you been?"

"To school."

"Bitch! Who told you to go to school? I'll beat you for that." I took off in a flash and ran all the way home.

That evening, when my father came home, he beat me. "I told you not to go to school, what do you mean by going to school? We don't have the money for it." He ranted on like that, and I cried all through his tirade. I wasn't able to do my homework, so I wasn't able to go to school the next day. My father terrified me. My calves had been beaten and beaten with a bamboo switch. I was sore and couldn't move; I just sat there crying.

One of my friends came by and said, "It's time for school."

"I can't go. My father will beat me." I sat there crying until my mother gave me some money on the sly and said, "Go to school before your father comes back." Without his knowing, I ran away to school. My father was on his way home for breakfast and I was on my way to school, so we passed right by each other. He grabbed my hair like this and said, "Go on! Go on!" meaning, "Go home," not "Go to school." I came back home.

He confronted me again. "Don't you listen to what your father says? I told you not to go to school, how dare you disobey me?"

But my mother said, "What do you mean by beating this child and preventing her from studying?"

My mother and father fought it out then and there.

"Why can't she go to school?"

"Because I say she can't go."

As I remember it, Father gave Mom a beating for encouraging her child to disobey. When I saw this, I didn't want to go to school. I thought, "First

Father beat me and then when Mother sent me to school in secret, he beat her too. If that's the way it is, I don't want to go." I'd averaged 98 points on the test. I'd advanced to the second year and taken the test to advance to the third year, but I wasn't able to continue. I didn't go that day, I didn't go on the second day, I didn't go on the third day, and then the teacher came to our house.

"Why aren't you sending this child to school?"

"I wanted to send her but her father won't let her go. He beat her." My mother explained why I couldn't go.

"Well then, have this child bring her father to school. I won't accept the monthly fee, I'll buy her pens and notebooks, but you must send this child to school. She studies hard and has a good mind. Why shouldn't you send her to school? You must." Nowadays they pay tuition and student fees, but in those days, it was a monthly fee.

So I brought my father to the teacher.[3] He greeted the teacher respectfully since, after all, this was a teacher. The teacher launched right into it, "All you have to do is let the child come to school." Father said that he couldn't do it, said it was useless for a girl to study. Ahyu! What a strange father, what a terrible father! The teacher said, "Think it over, discuss it with your wife, and then come back." I kept pestering Mom about it, but what could we do? My father would just keep beating me. So once again I went to school on the sly.

When my father came home, he would ask my mother where I'd gone.

"I sent her on an errand."

"Where did you send her?"

"Out to take care of something for me."

When I came home from school I couldn't do my homework because then my father would catch me. I was forced to do my homework in secret after my father had gone to sleep.

One day when I came home from school, my father announced that from then on I would have to work in the market when he came home for dinner.

"How can I sell things?"

"You do it so you'll have a living."

There was nothing I could do about it. I went out in the evening and went peddling until twelve o'clock. If you're doing business, everyone goes home by midnight. I went home and went to sleep, and then in the morning my father had already gone to the market when I got up. He didn't even come back for food and that was strange. This was when I finally had to stop going to school. My father told me to watch the store in the morning and do peddling in the evening, so how could I go to school? I simply couldn't go.

The children all wanted to know, "Why aren't you coming to school? Why aren't you coming to school?"

"My father won't let me. If I go to school he'll beat me."

"Your father's a bad man, really bad."

The other children were carrying their book bags and going to school but I couldn't go, I had to sell things. The other children were amazed. I sat there all alone and cried. One of my father's friends saw me and asked, "Why are you crying? What's the matter?"

"I'm crying because I can't go to school."

"Someone should beat your wretched dad to death."

Yongsu's Mother is well aware of her own sharp wits and continues to regret her lost education. Some months after this narration, we were poring over a household divination manual while she explained *kunghap,* the complex system used to determine the compatibility of brides' and grooms' horoscopes. Although the manual was written in vernacular Korean, this section included several long phrases in classical Chinese which stymied Yongsu's Mother. She began to complain once more about her wretched father who had not allowed her to study. If she had learned to read these characters she could earn more money by casting *kunghap.* This was only a modest and practical ambition, but one that had been bitterly lost.

Perhaps it was my introduction as "a student" that had appealed to Yongsu's Mother when she agreed to help me. She called herself my "shaman honorable teacher" *(mudang sŏnsaeng),* and this was true. There are "shamans" *(mansin)* and "great shamans" *(k'ŭn mansin),* and this usage was the source of a standing joke between us. "When you become a professor *(paksa),* Tallae, what will I be?"

"A great professor *(k'ŭn paksa).*"

I recalled this phrase when I wrote to inform her of my new Ph.D. The news of her "great professor" status was mirthfully shared with her *mansin* colleagues, who relayed the joke back to me when I returned a few years later.

The image of a forlorn child, left behind while others go off to school toting book bags, recurred in her laments over her daughter's early pregnancy. The Willow Market Daughter, raised by Yongsu's

Mother's sister, was still in her late teens when she entered a common-law union with an enterprising migrant from another province. The Willow Market Daughter was eighteen years old and pregnant when I made her acquaintance at Yongsu's Mother's house. Yongsu's Mother explained the situation with a wry smile—it was a case of "a baby having a baby." Her daughter should "still be carrying a book bag and going to school." The image pleased Yongsu's Mother and again she saw the loss. By the 1980s a few village sons and daughters were attending universities and Yongsu's Mother was relentless in her criticism of those who, she felt, abused the opportunity. Once, in recent years, she seemed to take some delight in lecturing my research assistants on the diligence and perseverance required to attain a Ph.D. in anthropology, embroidering her observations of my early fieldwork into a moralistic tale.

Like Yongsu's Mother, the six shamans that Harvey interviewed "had inordinate difficulty in reconciling either cognitively or emotionally the discrepancies they perceived between social expectations of them as women and their personal goals and interests as individuals. They were critical of cultural norms others accepted as givens in their lives, were hypersensitive to cultural inconsistencies, and suffered from a deep and abiding sense of having been morally injured as human beings" (Harvey 1979:236–237). But while Harvey's six informants were abused or disappointed in their married lives, and generally recall more pleasant childhoods, Yongsu's Mother describes injustice as an early memory. Her unabashed dislike of her father is also unusual, both when compared with Harvey's six *mansin* and with more general Korean expectations. The Korean father-daughter relationship is usually affectionate, albeit touched with ambivalence if an admired father mistreats a beloved mother (ibid.; Han 1949:119; Kendall n.d.a). For most of the women in Harvey's study, fathers were benign and relatively distant figures. The one informant who expressed anger felt betrayed when her formerly indulgent father married her off against her wishes (Harvey 1979:49–52). Yongsu's Mother's betrayal came early, but the belligerent man would reappear in other guises throughout her story. As for her father, the worst was yet to come.

I stopped going to school. I just sat there obediently in the shop and sold things. Then something odd happened. I saw my father in the market. He bought some fish and then he bought some meat and went on his way. When I went home I asked my mother about it, but she said that he hadn't brought anything home. He hadn't even come home himself. This was a strange turn of events. I ate my dinner and went back out, and then my father came back from dinner later.

My father was so frightening that we children weren't able to eat in his presence. If he was there, we couldn't sit with our ankles crossed. We even had to set our kimchee on the floor and eat it from there; we weren't allowed to place our own food on the tray. He was a terror. When we had fish, he ate all the flesh, and then didn't the rest of us get just the head? He was so strict that we weren't even able to eat the fish head when he was there. And we couldn't eat the white stalks of the cabbage leaves in kimchee. We could just eat the bare, leafy parts, and only at floor level. And if the meal tray appeared without side dishes, well then he'd just send it back in a flash, complaining. That was why Mom spent so much time worrying about Father's food. But we weren't allowed to eat those things.

Even so, it was strange that he had bought fish, dried covina fish, and then when I asked Mother about it, he hadn't brought the fish home to her. Strange, strange. I became very shrewd. I ate my meal and went back to the shop. "Father, please go and have your meal."

"Fine, watch the shop."

As soon as my father had left, I asked one of his friends, "Please watch the shop. I have to go after my father."

"Why? What do you mean by chasing after your father?"

"Uh, I've got to catch him, so please, Uncle, watch the shop for me."

My father was already well ahead of me. I followed him secretly, wondering where he was going. He bought fish and things again and went on. This time, I stayed right on his trail. Our house was this way but he turned down an alley in the opposite direction. That was yet more strange. So I followed him down the alley. My father didn't have the least idea that I was following close behind him. He went into a house, a house with a galvanized metal roof, he went right inside, carrying his purchases. Once he had gone through the front gate, I crept up quietly and stood outside. I heard someone say, "Father's here, Father's here." That was stranger still. [From what follows, the child in the house would have been too young to speak. The speaker could have been the woman addressing her child, but Yongsu's Mother used a childish voice and phrase, perhaps again for effect.]

I went back to the shop. I watched the shop and mulled over what I had seen.

After a while, my father returned from eating.
"Father, have you eaten?"
"Yes, I have."
I looked after the store with my father and then he sent me home. When I got home, I didn't say a word to my mother. I thought that it would make her anxious. I just brooded over the strangeness of it all, not able to talk about it. My brother was studying, and I had to go back to the store once I had eaten dinner. When I returned again, "Brother, Brother, wake up."
"Why'd you wake me up? You're going to pester me to death."
"Get up and listen to me. Our father went to the iron-roofed house, to the house in the alleyway just below the hospital. He bought fish and brought it to the iron-roofed house. I heard somebody in there call him 'Father.' I followed him, and this is what I found out."
"Retard! You don't know what you're talking about. So what if Father goes into some stranger's house?" My brother just bawled me out.
"It's true. I saw it all clearly."
"Go to sleep, retard, go to sleep."
He couldn't comprehend it. In fact, my brother didn't even hear what I was saying.
The next evening my father said, "I'm going to leave early tonight. Go home when you've sold everything."
"Yes," I said, but I just left the produce there. So what if someone walked off with it? I chased after him again. He turned into that same house again. Strange, why should he go into that particular house? Well, I went back, set out some more things, and sold them all, and when I was done I went back home.
My mother said, "You're back already. Why hasn't your father come home yet?"
"He's not coming. He went out drinking somewhere." Even though I knew otherwise, I couldn't say anything to my mother so I told her this business about his going drinking.
"Ahyu! Bastard liquor," she muttered. "Let's go to sleep." But you have to be able to sleep, and I just kept fretting. It was odd that my father had gone into that house.
After a while, my father came back. My mother went out and opened the gate. She asked him why he was so late.
"I went out with my friends and there was some drinking." But he didn't seem the least bit drunk.
"Has the child come back?"

"She's come back. She's already asleep."

At least he didn't know what I had done. I fretted about what I should do. My father went in and went to sleep. He left again at dawn. I went out myself a little bit later, but one of my father's friends saw me.

"Who are you chasing after? Where do you think you're going?"

"Who, me?" If I said anything to my father's friend and then if he should tell my father, my father would beat me to death. I mean he'd really kill me. A wench of a girl shouldn't reveal such things.

I followed after him several times, all by myself. At home my father didn't buy us anything for side dishes, and he brought us only a little rice. The only person I could tell was my brother. I had thought it through and decided that there was nothing else to do. I decided to make my brother tag along with me. That evening, I caught him as he passed the shop on his way back from school.

"Sit down, sit down."

"I've got to go and do my homework."

"Have a seat first. You'll soon see why it's important."

My father saw my brother and asked, "What are you doing here?"

"I came out for the fresh air."

The two of us just sat there until my father shut the door of the shop and went out. Then my brother and I followed behind him in secret. We followed him to that house and he went inside. He had gone to the butcher and bought some meat, and then he went to that house again. The two of us saw everything, my brother and I.

My brother said, "This is horrible. From now on, neither of us will be able to study. I won't be able to study either. What are we going to do?"

We didn't know what we should do. Hours passed, and then at midnight, we went back home. We'd done all that we possibly could. Mother didn't know a thing about it and we didn't tell her. She thought that he was just out drinking and that was why he came back late. But then one day she said, "Ahyu! Does your father have any business at all these days? He should give us more money to live on."

Having said it, she fought with my father night and day.

"The money's all spent. There's nothing I can do about it."

"I need money for rice and firewood and coal."

"I told you, business is bad. You're just carrying on." And with that, he got up and left. He left, and after that our household wherewithal gradually went to pieces. Bit by bit, he stopped giving us money and he stopped buying us rice and firewood. Most of the time, he just went to his little wife. We'd reached the crisis; it was time to tell Mother. "Father's taken a little wife and he's living there. That's why he isn't bringing us any money."

My mother was so furious she grew horns. "Let that old bastard just try to come back! I've had it! I'm through!" My father came back by and by, but this time he and my mother had a huge fight.

"Even if you've gotten yourself a little wife you have to feed us. Why should we starve to death while that woman eats?"

She fought him, but now my father was angry. Now he didn't even come to our house. He preferred it that way since we knew. Now he ran the store alone; he told me not to help him anymore. I think he suspected that I'd give the money I made to Mother. It takes money to get by. Do you think we had rice to spare? One morning Mom didn't cook breakfast. "There's no rice. Take this sack to your father. Go to your little mother's house."

I went. This first time I just went. "Is my father there?"

"Who are you?"

"It's me!"

"Who's me?"

"Isn't my father in there?"

With this, she opened the door and took a look at me. I'd never seen that woman before and she didn't know who I was. There was a tiny baby in her arms, a baby that had passed the first hundred days and was well on its way to the first birthday.

I said, "Ahem, doesn't Mr. Pak N——who trades in the market come here?" I told her his name and she admitted that this was the right place. "Where has Father gone?" He wasn't back yet from the market. I said I would wait, and I waited. I'd come to ask for rice so I waited until my father came back. He opened the door and came in.

"Father!" He was startled. He stood there in shock wondering how this girl had known where to find him. "Father, give us rice. We don't have anything to eat, the grain's all gone."

"I'll beat you to death, girl! I'll kill you! How did you know to come here?" He rushed at me to beat me. He brandished a stick of firewood and said he'd kill me. What could I do? I fled outside. He'd beat me. I fled as far as the threshold of the front gate and sat down, then I went back inside. Now my temper was up.

"Father, give me rice."

My little mother raised a fuss, she raised such a fuss that my father picked up his stick again and chased me out. I fled back home. I told Mother that Father was going to beat me.

"Shame on him. What's the use? If we're going to starve to death, well then we'll starve to death. Don't go back there."

"My stomach is empty. Don't tell me not to go, I'm going." I was in a daze. A little bit later I went out again. This time I went to the shop. My anger was up. I clutched the sack and went to the shop. "Father, buy us rice."

My father's friends were there as well as the people doing business, so this was embarrassing for him.

"Buy us some rice." I stood there clutching the sack.

"Come here." I followed him. He bought some rice and gave it to me, just a little bit of rice. Even so, I took this and went right home. I gave it to my mother and said, "Fix some food."

She cooked the rice and we ate. We ate some for breakfast the next day and then the rice was all gone again. I went out carrying the sack. When I went to the little mother's house, my father said that he was going to beat me to death. It was that way the first time I went, the second time, and the third time. Finally, exhausted, I went back once more and the little mother said he wasn't there. So, once again, I went to the shop.

"Buy us some rice. Buy us a measure of rice."

He bought a measure of rice and gave it to me.

"Buy us wood. We don't have any firewood either." He bought a bundle of firewood and gave it to me. I brought these things back home. Every day, morning and evening, I went out and asked my father to buy us rice. I went to the little wife's house. After a while, I got tired of it, and told my brother, "You go," but my brother just said, "I don't want to." "Well then, let's go together." The two of us would go and beg my father for rice. We couldn't live on what we brought back. We had difficulties for days on end, and my stomach was empty. I told you how I would eat at the factory boss's house [see below].

After a while, my brother graduated from school and he joined the Homeland Reserve (Hyangt'o Yebigun). He went into the youth division and was trained when he was fifteen. When the Korean War war broke out, my brother joined the army. He was eighteen years old when he went into the army and my elder sister had been eighteen years old when she got married. There were just four of us in the household during the war, my mother, my younger brother and sister, and I.

The girl Changmi was born into a family of petty entrepreneurs, recent urban migrants. The fruit stall in the market parallels, on a far smaller scale, the many fruit and vegetable shops opened by Korean immigrants who arrived in New York City in the 1970s and 1980s with some funds and a wealth of family labor. The father's business would have required an initial investment and then long hours of steady work. Like other urban women in precarious circumstances, the mother vended foodstuffs made at home or hawked water from door to door, occupations that would provide some remuneration but no great profit.[4] In widowhood, Yongsu's Mother would make a slim livelihood through similar means.

Changmi's parents, born, raised, and wed in the countryside, were among the early wave of migrants who flooded Korean cities during the colonial period. Pushed by population pressure on the land and pulled by the lure of new urban opportunities, the colonial migrants initiated a pattern that would overwhelm Korea's cities in the decades after the war. Yongsu's Mother's family history thus parallels the precarious existence of many of the women who came to her shrine in the 1970s, the wives of small shopkeepers, market vendors, day laborers, and semiskilled workers.

Although her parents maintained ties with the husband's rural relations, distant kin offered little protection when Changmi's father abandoned his wife and children to near starvation. The city freed him from the moral coercion of parents, brothers, and uncles. His rural kin would publicly shame him, years later, but this seems to have been a solitary gesture. Changmi's mother, purchased by her husband's family and raised in their home as an adopted daughter-in-law *(minmyŏnŭri),* lacked recourse to her own natal kin.[5]

The concubine was also a product of the city, a woman who had fled a disagreeable marriage. Yongsu's Mother knew the prior history of her father's little wife, or perhaps she was able to fabricate from a common pattern of little wives. This is a paraphrase from my field notes.

The little mother was the only daughter in a family with five sons. They married her off in style with a huge chest filled with clothes. But she didn't like her husband, so she came back home again, already pregnant from her marriage. Her mother, fierce as a tiger, said, "Whether you live or die, you belong in your husband's house; you can't come back here." She went to work in a wine house, and my father got a look at her while he was in his cups. The proprietress told him that the woman had run away from her husband's house and that she'd just had a baby. He set her up in a house, all in secret, without letting my mother know, and then later she had a baby by my father. There were two daughters, but one died.

The little mother is still alive. She must be about fifty-seven years old, and if my father were alive, he'd be seventy-seven. She came to my mother's sixtieth birthday *(hwan'gap)* and they posed for a picture together wearing identical Korean dresses. I looked at them and laughed, two wives without a husband between them.

Although Yongsu's Mother implies that the father forced the girl to tend shop to facilitate his own extended philandering, the girl's education ended around the time of her sister's marriage. Perhaps she was pulled into the shop to take the older girl's place. Nevertheless, a choice was made and the dull son's education continued at the expense of his more intelligent sister, a choice that followed cultural logic—the son would have far greater need of an education—but confounded the daughter's sense of her own worth.

The elder sister, who figures so prominently in Yongsu's Mother's adult life, is remarkably absent in the stories of her childhood. When I asked specifically about her, Yongsu's Mother commented bluntly, "She was gone," although she would have been part of the household during the first nine or ten years of Changmi's life. On another occasion, Yongsu's Mother remarked, with some resentment, that by marrying early her sister had escaped the grim years that followed their father's desertion. It was Changmi who worked herself to the bone.

When I was thirteen years old, I went to the printing factory. This was before the Korean War. I was so hungry that they often gave me food at the boss's house. That shows what a good worker I was. The boss was very fond of me. He'd say, "Won't you come over and have something to eat?" If I fell asleep, he would know that I hadn't eaten and would tell the cook to give me some food.

How did I get that job? The neighborhood section chief's *(panjang)* sister was married to the man who ran the factory. The section chief looked after all the neighbors' business. He told me that if I went to work in the factory and learned a skill, then I would be able to earn a living and buy food. Well,

I stayed there for seven years, from the time I was thirteen until after I was twenty. The boss even gave me the key. That was because I'd been there for so long.

Does she romanticize the boss's kindness to compensate for the cruel treatment she received from her own father? Her accounts of the benevolent factory boss are at least consistent, repeated throughout the stories of her working life, although she does complain about the low pay (chapter 5).[6] Around this same time, Changmi joined the Korean Youth League (Taehan Ch'ŏngnyŏndan), whose paramilitary drills she recalls with zest.[7]

The league would train every morning from six to seven, and in the evening from seven to eight [or eight to nine]. "Forward, retreat, hit the ground." We had a sentry at our headquarters who worked day and night, "Forward, retreat, hit the ground." Every day I shouldered a gun and did sentry duty. We did sentry duty in shifts at the headquarters. We stood guard outside and there was a password. If anyone came by while we were standing guard duty, we'd point our guns at them and demand the password. Those who could give the password were members of our organization and those who couldn't weren't. We had the place completely encircled. "Password!" If they couldn't answer, then it was "Shoot!" If they couldn't answer, you'd pull the trigger, right then and there. That was how tough the members of our organization were when they stood guard.

Well, our chief wanted to check up on us to see whether or not we were being thorough, so he came by and stood there without giving the password. I pulled the trigger to alert our members and they all rushed to the defense. Then we saw it was the chief, ha, ha.

Many Koreans, even those who were children in 1945, remember the liberation as a high tide of optimism and celebration. Liberation Day, August 15, 1945, has become historical shorthand for the complex events and powerful emotions that marked Korea's emergence from colonial rule. Yongsu's Mother ties her own history to this key event, but for her the time of national liberation is associated with the onset of personal hardship, the end of her education, and her father's betrayal. With the outbreak of the Korean War, worse was to come.

FOUR

War Stories and a Meeting with the Mountain God

The Korean War gouged a bloody swath across the youthful reminiscences of Yongsu's Mother's generation. Every year, as the ominous date of June 25 approaches, images of death and destruction, snippets of vintage newsreels and myriad replays of old war movies flutter across the television screen in many a Korean household. Among the viewers, those who remember tell their tales, invoking old fears and uncertainties for those who were raised in a time of peace. In Yongsu's Mother's remembrance of June 25, 1950, the bombs, flames, and corpses are the horrible background to her father's worst betrayal.

Everyone else fled, but did we have anything to eat? Did we have any money? We couldn't flee anywhere. We couldn't escape. My little brother, my little sister, and I were sobbing, crying, "Let's escape!" My mother said, "We don't have a scrap of food. What will we do if we go away? If we're going to die, let's at least die at home."[1] But we kept crying and urging her to go. I should have gone south with members of the Korean Youth League. I had discussed it with my parents but "How can a girl go off traveling in a group?" They wouldn't let me go.

We cried all night, and all night we urged our mother to leave. But there wasn't anything to eat. My mother went somewhere and brought back a measure of parched wheat. She ground it round and round in the mortar and cooked it. She said that if we were going to flee, then we would have to eat something first. We were so hungry we cooked up that stuff and ate it. Then we rolled up our quilts and clothing to carry on our backs. My younger brother was small enough to ride on top of a bundle of clothing on my mother's back. I carried a bundle of clothing on my back, I carried our best rice pot on my back, I took my little sister by the hand. The parched wheat porridge that we had eaten gave us indigestion. My stomach hurt so much that I thought I would go crazy; it pitched and rolled. Even so, I was determined to flee.

We were on our way out when my mother said, "We can't go. We have neither food nor money. We'll go to your father." We kept after Mother all night, so that at dawn we all went over to the little mother's house. When we got there, they were eating roasted pork on white rice. My mother said that we had eaten parched wheat and that our stomachs hurt. My father's belly was full enough. He was annoyed that we hadn't all croaked. As for inviting us to try some of the white rice, he said not a word. They just went on eating. My younger brother, the one who's thirty-one years old now, was just three or four years old. He wanted to eat some of that food! Of course, they didn't give him any. They were the only ones who ate, my father and his little wife. When they had finished eating, we went out, all of us, with my father, my father's little wife, and her child. We went out together and eventually we got to the river.

We were too late. The bridge had been cut. The planes were flying around dropping bombs everywhere. How could we cross? There was no way. The little mother's family lived in It'aewŏn, near Samgakchi, so we went there. When we got to her parents' house, the concubine's own mother grabbed my father and said, "Why have you cut yourself off from those kids of yours and attached yourself to our daughter? You should let her go. You're a real bastard, aren't you? You're not even scum, living with two women this way. Leave our daughter here with us. Take your own family and get out of here." My father's eyes rolled back. The planes were dropping bombs, the guns were firing, there was a real racket, and it was getting dark. He told us all to go out there and die, "Bitches, get out of here! You can't stay. Go drop dead."

My mother fought with him, "How can you chase us away?" But then she said, "All right, let's go home. As soon as it's light we'll go home. If we die, we'll die at home." There wasn't anything for us to eat the next morning either. In the dawn, still hungry, we packed up our bundles on our backs again. I took up my bundle of clothing and led my little sister. My mother put my little brother on her back, and we came back home again. If we were going to die, we were going to die at home. We came back hungry, without any breakfast. The People's Army, the reds, were already in the city. What could we do? Nothing.

From Samgakchi to Seoul Station, the ground was littered with bodies.

We had to step over them to make our way; there was no other path. The dead were everywhere. Overhead, the planes were dropping bombs. My father had told us to go and die. Well then, we were going home to die. We didn't have anywhere else to go.

Ahyu! On the way back, we saw a warehouse that had been opened. Barley, rolled barley, and Anamese rice had been piled up inside. One side of the warehouse was already on fire.

How was it opened?

The People's Army opened it. Or, no, the National Army opened it as they retreated. They left it when they retreated so that the People's Army wouldn't gobble it up. They left it for the people to eat.

Questioned, she catches herself, lest she say anything good about the reds. In another, uninterrupted telling, the reds opened the warehouse.

The bombs were falling from up above. My mother said, "Take the kids home and stay there; I'm going to carry off some of that grain."

"Mother, you can't go. They're bombing. You'll die if you go in there!"

"I've got to get some of that grain, even if it kills me. Then you'll all have something to eat and we'll survive. Don't you see? Your father sent us out to die in the bombing, but aren't we more likely to starve to death? Let's haul away some of that stuff so we can eat."

The bombs were falling and the bullets were flying. My mother hauled out some barley and some flour, three sacks worth, and we carried it back. For the first time there was something to eat. For the first time we could cook some food and eat it. With the flour we made dumplings and noodles, and with the rolled barley we made porridge. Now we had enough to eat! My mother had carried out three or four sacks worth.

We got home, but the planes were bombing and making a racket. We would go down into the bomb shelter and come back out again, back and forth. This was still going on when my father showed up at the house. There he was. My mother asked him, "What do you mean by coming back?"

He told us that his mother-in-law (the little wife's mother) had raised such a fuss that he couldn't stay there, so he'd come back. That's what he said. He'd come back. My mother had snatched rolled barley and flour when the bombs were falling, and now we had plenty to eat. Now the old man told me, "You go to It'aewŏn and bring your little mother back, even if you have to lead her on a string. Go out into the fray and bring her back."

I walked. If I didn't obey he wouldn't let me have anything to eat and would beat me to death besides. He chased me out and I went. They were bombing over toward It'aewŏn now. First I hid myself here, then I went on and hid myself there, and made my way.

"Little Mother!"

"What do you want?"

"My father sent me for you."

"I won't go."

"He wants you to come right away."

"So what? I won't go. Don't even mention it."

That bitch was too much! I went back home. "The little mother says she won't come."

"Typhoid take you, girl! I told you to bring her back. What do you mean by coming back alone?"

Once again he threatened to beat me to death, this time because I hadn't brought the little mother back. I went again, again!

"My father wants you to come."

"I said I wouldn't go. What do you mean by coming back?"

I lost my nerve and went back home again. "The little mother says she won't come. She says it's useless for me to fetch her. She simply won't come."

Then he chased me out with a stick and said he'd kill me. "I told you to drag her back if you had to. What do you mean by coming back alone?"

I went and called her, and the little mother came. My mother, father, and the little mother all lived together. Then our father saw that we were running out of food, that there were only about five measures of barley left. He and our so-called little mother took it and the two of them snuck away together without a trace. [In the telling she pantomimes their carrying the bag between them as they ran.]

They fled to the country. They left us without anything to eat. Didn't they just! My father took it all and ran away. What could we do? Now we really went hungry. We bought chaff and ate that, chaff! They used to sell wheat chaff. We'd buy that and make coarse pancakes or dumplings, but after a while we didn't even have the money to buy chaff. Then we were hungry, hungry all the time. I was so hungry that I would even eat the dross from the soy sauce, the remainder after they've steeped the malt. I was so hungry I ate that whenever I could get ahold of it. When I closed my eyes, all I could see was food.

Around that time, the "Western prostitutes" *(yang kalbo)* appeared.

There was an auntie who used to peddle fruit and things around the military base who wanted me to go around with her because I could speak some English . . . Oh no, but the Americans weren't here then! I mean that my father ran away when the People's Army was here. We were eating, my mother, my brother and sister, and I; the four of us were eating coarse barley pancakes, kimchee, and cabbage soup when the People's Army men burst through the door with their guns pointed and told us to raise our hands.

She had gotten ahead of herself as one hungry memory followed another. Coarse barley pancakes were a link to a wartime tale, and she began with a remembered meal, an undistinguished meal, but a veritable feast in contrast to the lean days that would follow.

They told us to come out with our hands raised. They let my brother and sister stay behind, they only seized my mother and I. They took us both with them, but they sent my mother back home. They had nabbed me, and they took me along with them to their headquarters. The woman who lived just down the slope from us had informed on me. She had been living with a People's Army man; she was the one who had squealed.

Why?

I worked with the Korean Youth League (Taehan Ch'ŏngnyŏndan), in the opposition, and my brother had joined the National Army; that was why. They held me in their headquarters. I was there for a long time without anything to eat. There was nothing but chaff. They made our food with that; they would add just a little bit of salt and roll it into a ball, like a rice ball. That was what they gave us to eat. Since there wasn't any rice to eat, even at home, I ate what they gave me.

Then the People's Army interrogated me. Did they ever put me through it! "Isn't your brother with the National Army?"

"That's not so. I don't have an elder brother. I don't have an elder sister. I'm the eldest daughter. How can I have an elder brother in the army?"

"Your brother's in the army and you work for the opposition. Isn't that so?" [. . .][2]

"What sort of work could I do? I'm young and my family's poor. I wasn't even able to go to school. I didn't do anything."

"Why are you lying to us?"

They clicked their guns and clicked them again, and kept after me. They said they'd shoot. Well, let them shoot. If I should die, that's all there was to it. But if I told them that my brother was in the National Army and that I worked for the opposition, they'd call me a reactionary element *(pandong punja)*. Then wouldn't these bastards kill our whole family! [. . .]

They told me I was being stubborn, but there was nothing they could do about it. All I would say was that it wasn't so. I spent the night there, and each wretch that came in interrogated me. Each wretch that came in would snarl and threaten me. "If you don't talk, we'll kill you." This went on all night. They kept on interrogating me, and I was scared. And all night my mother walked back and forth in front of the gate, her hair all unbound, wondering if I was dead or alive.

On the evening of the second day they said, "If you want us to send you home, then talk." They'd given me neither food nor water, and I was so hungry that I thought I'd die. I'd reached my limit. I knew that I could easily make a slip and die at their hands. I felt faint; I was fading in and out. They were really vexed. [. . .]

"Let's take the kid home."

We went to my house, and all the way they kept their guns pointed at me. My mother grabbed me and cried. "Shh, they're out there." They'd brought me home so that they could eavesdrop on whatever my mother and I might say to each other. I told her not to say anything.

"You must be really hungry. Eat something." She'd gotten barley grain and cooked it. I ate one spoonful and was just about to eat another when that bastard threw open the door.

"Come out here. What have you and your mother been saying to each other?"

"I haven't said anything. I haven't the strength. My mother just gave me some food and I ate."

He told me to come out, and then that guy ate up all the food, the People's Army bastard! He took it away from me and ate it because he was hungry too. My mother was heartbroken. Even though there wasn't any food to spare, she'd set this aside, hoping that I might come back so she could feed it to me. And now that bastard had eaten it! When he'd finished every last bit, he told me to get going. There was nothing I could do but go back with them again. They forced me along, and once again,

"What were you talking about with your mother?"

"I didn't say anything. I was hungry. My mother gave me something to eat. I ate, that was all. What was there to talk about?"

Then pow! He slapped me. "I've never seen such a stubborn little girl." [. . .]

I was interrogated all night. I was interrogated for three days. By the third day, I was exhausted and famished. One of those bastards picked up his gun and yelled at me. [. . .]

I slumped against the desk. "Stand up! If you listen to us, you can go home, live with your mother, eat something. Why won't you say anything? We're going to have to kill you."

I had nothing to say. I didn't have the strength. I was going to die.

"Come out here. We're going to shoot you because you didn't talk." They forced me out again, told me where to go and I went. They took up their guns and fired at the wall beside me. I was petrified, absolutely petrified. I sank down, plop. I mean, I'd been standing there and a bullet went off, *p'aeng,* right at my side. What could I do? I thought that I was dead. I slumped down and blacked out. Then that bastard told me, "Get up!" and I got back up again. And once more they questioned me, demanded that I answer, said that they would have to kill me. They dragged me back to the office. There I was again. They had dragged me back and now I got my fourth day of interrogation.

It was the evening of the fifth day, midwinter, when it's already dark by six o'clock and you can't see anyone approaching from a distance.[3] As if from nowhere, they brought in all of the people that they'd seized, those bastards. How had they managed to grab so many people? Maybe now they were really going to shoot me. I was giddy, giddy; I saw one person as two, then three. I was really in a state. They called me and forced me out, dropping with exhaustion. They made everyone stand in a line and placed me in the middle. I couldn't fathom what was going on. I was numb. I hadn't washed my hair, I hadn't washed my face, I was black with dirt and tears, filthy beyond recognition. I looked like a beggar standing there. An old man, a grandfather who had also been seized, asked me, "Child, where did they capture you?" [This is the first kind "grandfather" of the piece.]

"I live over there."

"But why have they seized you and brought you here?" He asked me this in secret.

"They say that I'm a reactionary element and that they're going to kill me. So here I am, and it looks like I'm really going to die."

That grandfather said, "Ahyu, it's pitiful. What can we do? What sort of fiends kill children?"

A little bit later, the commander arrived and shouted at us to stand in a straight line. That chattering fool seemed to be saying that we would be taken to the North, but if we should try to escape, we would be shot. We shouldn't even think of escaping. If we obeyed we would survive, and once we got through this, we'd live in nice houses, wear good clothes, and have a lot to eat; we'd have a good life.[4] So those bastards were going to drag us away to the North.

Years after the telling of this tale, working with tapes and transcripts, I was uneasy. My goal, to record an appreciation of Yongsu's Mother as a storyteller, seemed both justifiable and sufficient when she described her own life against a general background of Korean society and culture. As an anthropologist, I could easily accept the cultural validity and personal truth of Yongsu's Mother's gods and ancestors, accounts which resonated with spirit possession motifs from Korea and many other places. I was less sanguine about the reds, for here Yongsu's Mother collides with history and contributes to the oral record of significant events. Speaking thirty years after the history she describes, is she an accurate witness?

Beginning in August of 1950 there were massive roundups of suspected rightists, including leaders of the Youth League, many of whom were fingered by informers (Riley and Schram 1951:89). Although she never claimed to be a "leader," I had assumed that she was picked up at this time. When I questioned her on this point in 1985, however, she told me that she was taken when the People's Army made their final retreat from Seoul in 1951. Yongsu's Mother follows other survivors' testimonies in her descriptions of the meager prison fare and the coercive necessity of confession. These same sources, however, suggest that not even prominent rightists received the constant grilling she describes. Would the People's Army, facing serious military reverses, have expended so much energy, even staged a mock execution, to extract a confession from a fifteen-year-old girl? If she had more to confess than the simple business of running errands and playing soldier, this is not a part of her tale. The story of her capture is no less fascinating than the rest of her account, but her listener could not resist a ripple of cynicism. To what degree was her account colored by the incessant anticommunism of prime-time Korean television? (To what degree are my own doubts prompted by my thorough impatience with this genre?) Like tales of Princess Pari and images of Mountain Gods, interrogations by villainous communists are a part of the imagery available to the contemporary Korean storyteller.

In the fall of 1985, still nagged by these questions, I asked her mother about their experiences during the war. Yes, she confirmed, Yongsu's Mother had been captured and saved by the Mountain God. The People's Army took all the young people in the neighborhood, and the rest had died at the Imjin River. A childhood friend was killed. Yongsu's Mother would tell me the story later; the girl had been shot while trying to escape, executed as an example for the rest of them. I asked Yongsu's Grandmother, "But wasn't there a woman red who lived with a People's Army man and who made trouble for you?" "Oh, that one," Yongsu's Grandmother smiled, perhaps because I knew the story. "They called me in, but when they saw that I had nothing, they let me go."

Could Yongsu's Mother have collapsed two experiences—a brief (but frightening) interrogation early on, and the ordeal of her capture at the time of the final retreat? Perhaps. As her annotator, I simply do not know where Yongsu's Mother's lived experience merges with a larger cultural memory of civil war. I heard the story of her interrogation twice, with the following tale told in sequence, but this next tale often stands alone. It is perhaps the most frequently recited tale in Yongsu's Mother's repertoire.[5]

They took us away in the night. This was probably because the National Army had already crossed the river, so they weren't able to move in broad daylight. I'd planned to escape during the journey, but it was impossible. The boy at the rear of the line got away, but if I tried to leave the middle of the line, they'd see that I was missing. Those at the back of the line could escape; they all got away in the dark without being caught.

We went in a line, forced along all night, and then when it got light, they took us to some abandoned house. Our guards hadn't brought so much as a grain of rice. There wasn't so much as half a sack of grain, maybe three or four *mal*.[6] If there was a pot, then they'd cook some of the grain, no more than a baby's fistful; they'd cook it up in salted water and that's what they gave us to eat. I was hungry; the first thing I thought about was food. The unhusked grain would pierce my stomach, but even so, it was something to eat and I ate. They poured the gruel into our cupped hands because there weren't any bowls; that's how they had us eat.

How many people were there?

Eighty people. During the day, we couldn't budge. Those wretches kept their eyes on everything that went on in the room. They posted a sentry in the doorway. They'd force us inside an empty house and then stand in the doorway. I couldn't escape from there. The sentry would threaten us with a stick of wood and bellow "Go to sleep!" Planes were flying around dropping bombs, so these People's Army bastards led us around at night and kept us inside the houses during the day. The planes were everywhere. So sleep. I lay down to sleep, but I lay down hungry. When it got dark, they'd give us another tiny bit of food in a ball and then lead us into the night and drag us on again. By the night of the third day, they'd run out of grain and didn't give us even that little bit of food. Those bastards were hungry and we were hungry. I was so hungry and cold that I could have died, I mean it.

It was the end of the third day, and I was sleeping. A white-haired grandfather appeared. A long white beard spilled down his chest and he stood up tall, holding a twisted staff, the staff that the Mountain God carries. The grandfather spoke [she draws out her words], "It's getting late; you don't have much time." What? I woke with a start. It was a dream. Everyone else was asleep. I was the only one awake, and I'd had that dream. My stomach was so empty, but I couldn't do a thing about it. I closed my eyes and settled down again. "It's getting late; you don't have much time." I woke up the girl who was sleeping beside me and told her my dream. "Let's escape! Whether we die in captivity or whether we die trying to escape, it's all the same. Let's get out of here."

If they caught us, we would be killed. She didn't even want to try. But if we were killed trying to escape, at least we wouldn't die burdened with regrets for our passivity.[7] But the other girl was afraid. How could we bring it off?

This girl still had some money, People's Army money, the money the reds used, printed with a rake and hoe.[8]

"What money is this?"

"It's what we use now."

"Where did you get it?"

"My grandmother and I were looking after the house [everyone else had fled]. I went out in the evening to see if I could buy some food, rice husks or wheat chaff or barley. Those people grabbed me and brought me here."

"Let's say we'll buy something to eat with this money and get out of here." I said this, but I had no idea where we were. We'd traveled by night and hidden ourselves by day. But I went to work on the other girl and coaxed her into it. We were about to get up when the guard came over with his stick and yelled at us to go to sleep.

"We have this money and we're so hungry that we can't sleep. Let us go out and get some bread."

"Absolutely not. If my superior finds out, then I'll really be in trouble."

"But if we go out and get a large chunk of bread, then you can have some and we can have some. We're so hungry we can't go on. Just let us go and buy bread and we'll come right back."

"No way. You'll just run away."

"Now look here, I was in your headquarters for four days and I've been on this march for four days.[9] It's already been a week, eight days. Have I escaped? Even if you threw me out, I wouldn't go. We'll buy some bread with this money and bring it back so we can all eat." [Arguing, she assumes the relentless nagging logic of the middle-aged woman, Yongsu's Mother. Now she becomes the girl again, back in character.]

The People's Army bastard seemed to think that was a good idea. He was hungry too. "Can you get back quickly?"

"We'll be right back, before anyone finds out about it." I insisted that the two of us would have to go together, so he let us both out. It was all because of my dream that I'd gotten up and talked about buying bread. That was why they let me go. It was all because I had Grandfather Mountain God's help, isn't that so?

We ran to the next village and peeked into a house, but it was deserted. We went to this house and it was empty, we went to that house and it was empty. Finally, we found an old woman in one of the houses.

"Grandmother! We were captured by the People's Army. We told them we were going to buy food. Can you hide us?"

She said that it would be too dangerous for her.

"We're hungry and want to buy some food."

"I don't have anything to spare."

"Grandmother, please give us something to eat. We're starving."

"Where do you come from?"

"We live in Seoul, but we were captured by the People's Army. We're so hungry. Can't you give us something, anything?"

"Children, you really must be starving." She had some barley pancakes in the kitchen, gorgeous barley pancakes. She gave us one this big. [She draws a full moon with her fingers.] She split it and gave a half to each of us. We ate it and took off, fled to the mountains.

We ran for our lives. Our feet stumbled on tree roots and our rubber shoes were torn into tatters. We fell and bled and cut our hands, but we kept on running. The day grew darker and darker; we didn't know what to do alone on the mountain, so we went back down to a village. We went to a house, but everyone had fled and the house was empty. We found an old-fashioned wardrobe cabinet that stood open on its hinges with the clothes spilling out. We went right over and looked inside. There was a pink skirt made of fine gauze. We tore it apart from the waist. The other girl took half and I took half. We were cold; we used it to cover ourselves. Each of us took her piece of cloth and crawled inside the cabinet to hide. We knew that if they caught us, we would die. We were hungry and cold. Before long, the two of us were sitting inside that cabinet crying. We cried for a while in the dark, and then fell asleep. I awoke with a start. It was already broad daylight, so once again we went up to the mountain and ran for it. We fled by day, and as soon as it got dark, we went into an empty house and slept.

We spent two nights that way, and on the third day, we reached the pass northwest of Seoul. Just at the base of the pass, there was an endless stream of refugees crossing over. Ahyu, what if I should see my own mother there? I sat down for a bit and then went to cross over, but the People's Army soldier who was standing at the barrier called me aside. My heart sank. He told me to hand over the chit that they gave people when they crossed over. Well, what could I do? I lied. "I came over with my little sister, carrying a bundle on my head. My little sister has the chit. That person coming up now from over there is my mother. I've come back to fetch the bundle that she's carrying."

"It's not allowed. You can't go through. Since your mother is on her way, wait here for your bundle."

What could I do? I was an escapee, and I'd lied trying to get across. There was a girls' middle school in front of the Ansan Elementary School. The two of us sat right down there and cried, I and the girl who'd escaped with me. We bawled. Our homes were just a little bit further on, but how could we get across? Oh, we wept!

"Are you as hungry as all that?" There stood a grandfather with a long black beard wearing a black overcoat. He asked, "Where do you live, crying like this?"

"We live over there, but they won't let us across. Besides, we're hungry."

"Look at me." He studied my face and said, "Aren't you N——'s daughter?" Then I recognized him. It was my father's friend! He hadn't been able to flee south. His family was hungry, so he had gone to his kinsmen in the country and was bringing back some rice. He asked me what I was doing there and where I had been. I told him how we had been seized and taken away by the People's Army and had run away back here. Because we had escaped, we couldn't cross the checkpoint so we were stuck here.

"Come with me." He took us to the mountain behind the school. He brought out two flour pancakes—this large [her hands draw a great, round circle]—from the pocket of his black coat and gave them to us; he gave us one each [unlike the parsimonious old woman who had split a single pancake in two]. We were overcome with gratitude, and how delicious that pancake tasted! The grandfather even took off his overcoat and gave it to me because I was cold. I said that I didn't want it, but he told me to put it on, that he would be all right because he was wearing padded trousers. I put on the overcoat and we followed this grandfather over the mountain. When we got to the other side, there was Yŏkch'on Prison right in front of us. We had crossed the mountain.

A People's Army soldier was standing watch in front of the prison. Those bastards would probably shoot us if we tried to run past that point. Uncle told us to get down on the ground and he sat himself down under a pine tree. [Only now does she call him "Uncle," the more likely term for her father's friend. By calling him "Grandfather," she seems to equate him with the succoring Grandfather Mountain God.] He kept watch so that he could tell us to run for it when the soldier went away. After a while, an officer came out. The bastard who was keeping watch stood at attention and gave a salute. "Go on, get out of here, run!" The soldier had his back to us and couldn't see, so we got away. The other girl and I ran like crazy out of there.

We got through. I was on my way home. I told the other girl, "Let's go to my house first. We'll ask my mother to give us something to eat and then you can go on to your house." But the other girl said, "I don't even know if my grandmother is still alive. I went out to get her some food when I was captured. I have to find my grandmother." The other girl lived in Ahyŏn-dong and I lived in Yŏkch'on. I said, "If we both survive, come and see me." She said that she would and I went on up to my house. The house just in front of ours had been bombed away. Would our house be bombed like that too? I climbed up the path and there, our house was standing! I rushed in shouting "Mother!" But no Mother's voice called back. A fire was crackling, *panjjak, panjjak,* in the kitchen, so I went and opened the kitchen door. My little sister was cooking rice in a tiny little pot. She was tending the fire, breaking up the tiniest twigs of kindling with her hands.

"Hey you, where's Mother?"

"My mother isn't here."

"It's me, me! Your sister!"

"My sister was taken away by the People's Army and killed."

I had been gone for a week and she didn't recognize me. I hadn't washed my face, I hadn't combed my hair, my clothes were filthy. I kept shouting, "It's me, me!"[10]

She ran away and came back with my mother. As soon as I saw her, I cried out, "Hide me, Mother, hide me! If they catch me, I'll die."

Mother hadn't even paused to put her shoes on. She ran to me in her bare feet shouting, "Are you a person? A soul? A ghost?"

"Mother, they didn't kill me. I'm not a soul or a ghost. I'm alive, hide me!"

"Are you really human?"

"Mother, honestly, I'm a living person. Now hide me quickly so I'll survive. Otherwise, I'll die."

But my mother said, "Since you really are alive, come here." I went. My mother grabbed me. Mother cried and I cried, then she half dragged me to the bomb shelter. All of the neighborhood uncles and aunties were there. The neighbors gathered around and asked, "Are you a ghost or a human?"

"I'm really alive. I'm so cold and hungry I could die. Don't make me talk."

All of the neighborhood uncles said that I was brave. "How did you manage such a bold escape?" They put some boiled water in a hot water bottle to warm it up and gave it to me. My mother brought a pallet and a quilt and spread them out. Where I had been cold and hungry, I felt the warmth of the quilt and the hot water bottle stealing over me. I didn't have the least bit of strength. I fell asleep. I slept for a bit, and then my mother woke me and said, "Eat some of this." She had brought me cooked barley. I was going to eat it, but the neighbors wouldn't let me because I had been hungry for so long that my bowels were parched. If I ate solid food now, something awful would happen. They told my mother to put some of the barley in a bowl and smash it up with water, so my mother smashed the rice grains into a paste and gave it to me, just a little bit. Because I was starving and dried out, they wouldn't let me have more than this. I ate, and then I simply toppled over and went to sleep. My mother stayed there while I slept. Once, she shook me awake. I asked her what she meant by that. She said that I had been screaming in my sleep, "Run! Run for it!" Since I was awake, she gave me some more of the watered barley paste, and when I had eaten, I lay back down again. I went on like this, eating continuously but just a little bit each time.

Then, on the morning of the third day [or fourth day], the National Army entered the city at ten in the morning. Wasn't I glad! I ran out of the bomb shelter shouting, "*Manse, manse!* Ten thousand years to the Korean

Republic!" After all I'd gone through with those bastards, now I was full of joy.

A soldier yelled at me to get back under cover. They were an advance force and there was going to be trouble. I got out of the way, but then I snuck right around to my house. My mother was worried, "You've escaped, but what if the People's Army is still around? You'd better hide again."

"Why should I hide? The National Army's here. I'm not going to hide."

Because her son had joined the army, my mother assumed that she would see him again, but when I'd been carried off by the People's Army, she'd thought that I was lost. Now the National Army had come back, so I would survive. My mother and I grabbed each other and cried, I mean we really sobbed. My younger brother and sister followed our lead and started bawling. We were all standing there crying when, *p'ing, p'ing,* the bullets started to fly. The People's Army bastards were hiding on the mountain behind us and shooting at the National Army. It was a fire fight. So once again, we ran out to the bomb shelter. But Mother wasn't with us. This was serious. I told my little sister, "Go get Mother. Do you want Mother to die? Go get Mother."

"Elder Sister, you go."

"If I go, there'll be trouble. If I'm captured, they'll kill me."

"I don't want to go! They're shooting out there. I don't want to go."

The neighborhood uncles asked me how I could send my sister out there again, and they reassured us that my mother would be all right. We were both too scared to go back out. But then we heard them say "Tong-gil's house has been hit." Tong-gil was my little brother; they meant our house! Inside the bomb shelter they were saying that my mother must have been killed. When I heard that, I ran out of the bomb shelter screaming and crying, "Mother, Mother!"

I ran back to the house. The door was gaping wide and the room was thick with smoke. That was all; I couldn't see a thing. I was shouting, "Mother, where are you? Mother, where are you?"

"What's this?" She stood up right in front of me. She had been lying on the floor in front of the open door, covered with a quilt. She had nearly been hit by that shell.

"Mother! What are you doing here? We thought you'd been killed. Let's get to the bomb shelter."

"What's that smell?"

"Our house has been hit. Come on, let's get to the bomb shelter."

"Huh? A shell hit us?"

"That's right. That's why the doorway is wide open and the room is full of smoke."

We could see where the shell had gone clear through the wall. What if my mother had been standing there? I grabbed her and took her to the bomb shelter. There was shooting and fighting all night. The next day it was quiet. The National Army had advanced, so we came out and went home to set things right. We found our flag and hung it up. In every house where there were still people, I told them to fly their flags since the National Army had returned. But one old grandfather said, "It's too early to fly the flag. If there are People's Army men hiding in the neighborhood and we fly our flag, then won't they come secretly at night and kill us? It's premature."[11]

"What do you mean, 'premature'?" The National Army's here and those red wretches won't be back. And even if they should stab us to death, they'll be captured. They're running away. Hang your flag."

He agreed. The flags flew and the National Army advanced after a big battle. But what were we going to do? You need food to live, after all. My mother rationed it out, a little bit at a time. [And she repeats her account of eating little bits of barley paste during her recovery.]

I was all torn and scratched, but now I could wash my face and change my clothes. I took a basin of water, but once I'd washed my face, the water turned black, so black that words can't tell it. I threw that water out and washed my face again, and again the water turned so black that words can't tell it. My mother told me that it didn't matter; so long as I'd survived, everything was fine. [. . .]

Yongsu's Mother often tells this tale, in long or short versions depending on the situation, but always with a description of the Mountain God who spoke from a dream and prompted her escape. I have heard the tale at least half a dozen times. I must now bite my tongue and draw a deep breath, resisting the temptation to chant along with the Mountain God, "It's getting late; you don't have much time." When my assistant and I first expressed an interest in Yongsu's Mother's past, she told us the story in a rush; it was something that she wanted us to know about her, something that made her exceptional, extraordinary. She told it again, some months later, to illustrate the sorts of things that happen to a destined shaman. On this occasion, she entertained a village audience while edifying me. In our sessions with my tape recorder, she gave me the two long texts that I have combined here. In June of 1983, when her television screen was awash with images of bombed and burning houses, corpses, and anguished refugees, Yongsu's Mother began to reminisce, drifting into her tale of the old man with the long white beard and twisted staff. The tiny grandmother who lives next door to Yongsu's Mother undoubtedly bested me in the number of times that she had heard this tale; she sat mesmerized by the television screen, seemingly deaf to the rush of Yongsu's Mother's words.

The Mountain God's appearance is a significant turning, both in the tale and in Yongsu's Mother's life, and she recounts her vision with the precision of an invocation, "A long white beard spilled down his chest and he stood up tall, holding a twisted staff, the staff that the Mountain God carries . . . 'It's getting late; you don't have much time.' " This, in part, is why she honors the Mountain God and makes periodic pilgrimages to Kam'ak Mountain. This, in part, is why she became a shaman. Against all odds, the girl had been saved. Her dream vision gives meaning to two otherwise inexplicable themes in Yongsu's Mother's life: why, amid the irrational horror of war, she, alone, returned and why, despite salvation, so many awful things have happened to her. Hers was the wretched and marvelous fate of a destined *mansin*.

Yongsu's Mother's story is both personal and nearly archetypal. Encounters with divine beings and spiritual guides while wandering in the wild are a common motif in Korean shaman biographies. The white-bearded Mountain God frequently appears, described much as he is portrayed in shrine and temple paintings. Yongsu's Mother's colleague, Chatterbox Mansin, told me that she was drawn to Kam'ak Mountain and a power-charged relationship with the Mountain God during the period of distracted wandering that preceded her initiation and other *mansin* have told of similar experiences, but unlike Yongsu's Mother, they were already god-descended women *(naerin saram),* destined shamans in the lunatic season before their initiation. They were governed by spirit voices and visions, or drawn by inexplicable compulsions to temples, shrines, and sacred mountains.[12] Yongsu's Mother, snatched away by the People's Army, was a feisty teenager, not yet marked by the symptoms of her calling. Only in retrospect does her early meeting with the Mountain God become the significant first chapter of a *mansin*'s career. I suspect that this is why the tale is so often told. If Korean women accept that there are real shamans, they also assume that sloppy performers gather where there is money to be made. The calling, recounted as dreams, visions, crazed wanderings, and miraculous or portentous events, testifies to the strength of a *mansin*'s personal gods and the sincerity of her practice. These stories, both familiar and individualized, legitimize a woman's claim to be a *mansin*. Her aura is probably enhanced when a scholar with a tape recorder formally records the tale. And yet the tale of the Mountain God seems to be based upon a harrowing experience. In contrast to the melodrama of her interrogation, the core story is riddled with unromantic details: tripping over tree roots until her rubber shoes were in tatters, the warmth of the quilt once she was safe, her meticulous descriptions of the always inadequate rations, the dirty bath water. It is a personal tale, interpreted through cultural motifs and presented, time and again, with a storyteller's panache. The long leisurely account that she gave me concludes with an act of revenge, a chilling account for which there is no verification apart from the lingering furor of her rage.

I was at home when the leader of the Korean Youth League came by. His family name was Pak and I was also a Pak, so he came by and sought me out. He'd returned with the Homeland Reserve (Hyangt'o Yebigun), it's like the Defense Corps (Pangwigun) today. He came by our house while he was making his rounds. Since I hadn't been able to flee in a group with the rest of them, he wanted to know if I was dead or alive and came looking for me. I went out to see who was there, and it was the chief. We grabbed each other and cried. I was so happy to see him that I just sobbed. He'd heard that I'd been taken away by the People's Army, but there I was alive. [. . .]

He asked me to go out with him to survey the neighborhood. Many of those who fled had left the grandmothers behind. Only the younger people had fled, assuming that they would soon be back. The chief had come to survey the neighborhood, to see how many grandmothers and grandfathers had stayed behind and were now starving. We went to the first section *(pan)*, the second section, the third section, the fourth section, the fifth section, the sixth section, the seventh section, and the eighth section, we went through them all. We found so many grandmothers on the verge of starvation; they had nothing left to eat because their sons and daughters-in-law had all fled. We would do what we could to keep them alive. The chief provided grain and told me to cook it up into a porridge. We cut a wooden barrel with an ax, set a millstone inside, washed it well, and we cooked porridge in that, rice and barley. We gave some to each house twice a day;

every morning and evening, we cooked up porridge in that huge kettle. I took it around in a bucket and every morning and evening I gave two big ladles full to the grandmothers, but just to the grandmothers who weren't able to fix their own food. Before long the sons and daughters-in-law returned, and I stopped going to those houses because now they had something to eat, didn't they? The sons and daughters-in-law sought us out and thanked us. As time went by I gave out less and less porridge.

Then one day, my mother whispered to me, "They say that woman who squealed on you is still around; she hasn't fled."

"What? She's still here?"

I'd thought and thought about who could have informed on me, and there was only that woman. She had lived with a soldier from the People's Army. She knew that I belonged to the Korean Youth League and she had probably reported to the neighborhood chief that my brother was in the National Army. I told the chief about her.

We went to her house, the chief, the police, and I. She was at home, she hadn't run away. She probably thought that I'd been taken away by the People's Army and killed. She was just sitting there with her hair all up in pins.

"Come out, bitch! [Again, the girl uses the strong language of the middle-aged woman.] You informed on me to the People's Army. I was nearly killed because of you." She tried to plead with me, but it was because she knew that she was going to die, not because she had any feeling for me. I accused her, "This bitch, she was living with a People's Army man and she told them that my brother was in the National Army and that I was working with the opposition. That's why I had such an ordeal." The chief told them to bring her to headquarters and tie her up. When I saw her there, all bound, I can't tell you how furious I felt. I slapped her on this cheek and that cheek. I pounded on her and shrieked, "Why did you tell them to kill me, you bitch? I didn't die after all. I came back alive."

The inspector came in, and he was fierce. He said this woman red would have to die. He had her beaten where she was, tied to a post in the office. They'd bound her with heavy rope, and now they flogged her with more of the same rope, but she didn't cry out, not one word. They took a soldier's camp cot and broke it up for the wood; they beat her with that. The wood broke with a snap, but even then she didn't so much as say she was in pain. She just stood there in silence. "How is it that you lived with a People's Army man and squealed on this child? [. . .] Shouldn't you pay the price for that?" And they beat her some more. She didn't even utter a word of pain; was there ever such a stubborn woman? That bitch, she could snatch and devour a hundred people, she was so stubborn. [As Changmi herself had been stubborn.] The water was boiling, *pok, pok,* in the kettle, and they poured that on her. Then they got a rise out of her. But even so, she didn't say anything.

They dragged her back to her house and searched. While they were checking the flue under the floor, something bumped as if one of the floor stones had twitched loose. They found a space underneath and brought out reds' money and People's Army uniforms. That woman had hidden them under there.

What happened to her?

They killed that one. They beat her to death with wood from an army cot. Do you think that if I had died she would have given it the least thought? She'd squealed on me, and she'd lived with a People's Army man. Oh, I was full of rage!

We brought the things we found under the floor to the police and they asked me to tell my story—how I was interrogated and seized and taken away, about my escape. I told them everything. The police officer said that I had been very brave for one so young and gave me a reward. He put some money in an envelope and gave it to me. I bought a mirror to hang in the Youth League headquarters but it was broken when they changed command.[13]

I continued to make porridge for the grandmothers and grandfathers, but then one day the sons and daughters-in-law and daughters were all back to take care of them. About this time the whole Youth League came back. Because my father had prevented me from fleeing south with them, I'd been captured and had so many hardships, and now they had all come back safe, every last one of them.

Later, the National Army came back and the Americans arrived, Canadians and Filipinos, too, but lots of Americans. Life went on. I went to headquarters every day, but was so hungry that I could die. My mother went out peddling clothing in the villages because we didn't have anything to eat. She brought back rice and barley grain; that was because no one had any cash.

Where did she get the clothing?

You could buy clothes in the market, surplus relief goods. By hawking them around like that we could just barely get by. Many people were destitute now. The police, the section chiefs *(panjang)* and the neighborhood chiefs *(tongjang)* were all involved in the rationing. They gave rolled barley, Anamese rice, and something they said was American grain, all sorts of things like that. I went to the neighborhood association *(tonghoe)* when they discussed it. They only gave rations to those who were really desperate. There were households that received just one measure and households that received two measures. [. . .]

I went to the office every day; I ran errands to spread the alarm and call people to meetings, until I got a job.[14] I told the chief, "I've got to go and earn some money, I've got to eat, so I'd better find a job," and he wished me well. I was so hungry I could die. [She returns to the memory of hunger that threads through all her other memories of growing up.]

FIVE

Buddha Ties

Weeping, the old woman grabbed the monk's wooden clapper from the shrine, knelt, and rocking back and forth, cried out, "*Namuamit'abul, Namuamit'abul.*" She tapped the wooden clapper with an urgency unknown in Buddhist temples as the *kut* swirled round her to its own rhythm. At Yongsu's Mother's next flower-greeting *kut,* a year later, they tossed a robe across the old woman's shoulders and she spun through the *kut,* wielding the *mansin* trident and cudgel. "Look at Mother go!" One of the women nudged my shoulder and chuckled. In the shrine she again claimed the wooden clapper, knelt, and rocked herself to her own chanting. The animated woman was Yongsu's Grandmother, the old woman with the leather face who often appeared at her daughter's house, said little, in contrast to her ever-talkative daughters, and was given to naps, snoring quietly on the warm floor. Whatever had possessed her?

That was her Body-Governing God.[1] You didn't know that our mother has such a powerful one. When it's strong like that you have to do its bidding or it gets its dander up and gets nasty. My mother hasn't held a *kut* for, has it been five years? She really should have one this spring, but she just brought some rice cake when I held my own flower-greeting *kut.* When you try to get by with just a little, you can make things worse. Her Buddhist Sage comes on strong, it's ravenous. My mother's Buddhist Sage has a huge appetite.[2]

And the circumstances of her mother's acquiring a Buddhist Sage with a huge appetite were the stuff of another story.[3]

My mother says that she went to work in a Buddhist temple because times were tough. She went to work as a cook, fixing and serving up the rice, and by and by she gave birth to my elder brother there. The Hall of the Law[4] was on this side and the room where my mother slept was on that side, and that was where the baby was born. While my mother was giving birth, a monk hit his wooden clapper (in the main hall).[5] The child was born, the first hundred days passed, and when the first hundred days were nearly over, my mother left the temple. My father had secured a room and she went there to sleep. Now she lived outside, but shouldn't she have visited that temple? Times were tough and she was poor. Without money (for offerings), she never went back.

They say that in my mother's natal home, my maternal grandmother honored the Buddhist Sage.[6] As her daughter, my mother should have also honored the Buddhist Sage, but she had never done this. Besides, she had worked as a cook in a Buddhist temple. That's where the Buddha is, after all, so there was even more reason for her to honor the Buddha. Every time she went for a divination they would tell her that if she made offerings then things would be all right. If she went to a shaman, or if some *posal*[7] came by, they would always say, "The Buddhist Sage is really strong in this house; you absolutely must make the proper observances." But it takes money to worship. She didn't go to temples; she didn't set down offerings. She simply said that that was how it was.

Well, since my brother was born in a temple, he grew up without the slightest illness or injury. He was all grown up, I was fifteen and he was eighteen, I was in the Korean Youth League and he was in the militia when the notice came telling him to report to the army. It was the year that the Korean War broke out. [She digresses, reminds me of her thwarted flight, how the Han River Bridge had already been cut, forcing them to return home.] In her dreams my mother would be climbing a mountain. There were great boulders and rocks and stones. She would go up there and cook rice. The meaning of her dream was absolutely clear. She was being told to make an offering *(nogu me)*. Even so, we were poor, and in those days my mother didn't even think about superstition.[8] There were seven who went to the army from our neighborhood, and of all these, only my brother was killed.[9] [She speaks of how she and her mother went to the training camp to see him off, carrying rice cake made from a single measure of dearly purchased grain. They missed him; his unit had already left for the east coast. Later, they heard from a friend that he would be coming home on leave.]

Then, one day, I was washing my hair on the porch. I'd drawn the water and was already lathered up. My mother had gone out and come right back in, "A letter from your brother!" We'd heard he was coming home on leave. Why should there be a letter? "Grab hold of yourself, Mother. Let me finish washing my hair." "Come on, tell me what it says." "I'm in the midst of washing my hair. Let me finish." As soon as I was done, I looked it over. It was a letter saying that he had died, the very letter. Back then I couldn't read very well and didn't make much sense of it. There was a learned grandfather who lived just down the slope from us, so I took that letter off to him. "Grandfather, Grandfather, we've received a letter about my brother. It doesn't say 'notification of death,' but rather 'missing,' as if they don't know where he's gone. Grandfather, tell me exactly what it means." "They probably thought that your parents would have a shock if they said 'notification of death,' so they just said 'missing,' but they mean someone who has died, don't you think?"

So my brother was dead. All those who had gone and joined the army with him were coming back on leave. They all came back, and only my brother was dead.[9] My mother was troubled, so upset. I took the notice to the Sixth Army Headquarters, where they verified that he had died. I went through all the red tape and once that was done, my mother realized what had happened.

[The story goes on, how she, herself, became ill and received medicinal water in a dream, how her only surviving brother injured his arm in school, how her mother's troubles were compounded by the father's desertion, and how, finally, her mother began to make scrupulous offerings.] Even now, in my mother's house, she keeps a bowl of clear water and a candlestick in the loft. On the seventh day of the seventh lunar month she sets out flour pancakes (for the Seven Stars), she sets out offerings on the first day of the year and greets the first full moon.[10] She sets them out on special days. She's old now and can do as she pleases, but she keeps it up, even though my brother is grown and has children of his own. [But Yongsu's Mother also believes that it was already far too late when her mother began these observances.] If my mother had been able to do things right, well then, lickety-split, she would have taken care of everything. She couldn't. If it's for your son, you don't delay. That's why she's so frustrated now. There's a time to sow, and if you don't get the shoots in, the rice doesn't sprout up. I mean, you reap what you sow. They were always telling Mom, "Do it, do it," and since she didn't there's no help for it now, no matter how she flails about.

My younger brother's her only living son, the only son for two generations, since my father was an only son too—our grandfather was one of three. But as for this only son of two generations, he's lazy, he doesn't want to work, and all he wants is his liquor. All right, he farms, but to do that you have to plow the fields and when there's a drought, like the one we're having now, you have to pump and bail water for all you're worth. He doesn't, and frustration's aged my mother. And then there's the daughter-in-law, always squawking through her beak. If my mother says anything critical, then there's bitching. So she holds it back and smolders inside. [. . .] If only my elder brother had lived, things wouldn't be this way. Even back then, everyone said that he was diligent. What a shame, a real shame.

With her brother's death, Changmi became the mainstay of her family, a responsibility she carried until her marriage at the relatively late age of twenty-six. She describes her hardships after the war.

I was so hungry I could die, and once again I went out peddling. I'd buy braised chestnuts, gouge the meat out with a knife, and sell them. When the people from the print company returned, I went back there and worked. All that time, there was no news of my father, not since he'd told us to drop dead.

I went to work in the print factory and that was wretched! I was there for a month and they gave me two or three hundred won for a whole month's work.[11] I was furious! This was my wage? I told my mother, "Mom, shouldn't I get another job since everyone's come back now?" In the daytime I'd work in the print factory and then, no matter how hard it was, I'd go out and sell roasted chestnuts at night. My mother couldn't go out and get a job so what could I do? My mother sold water from house to house, fetched it for the neighbors. I went peddling and between the two of us, everyone got by on rice gruel. We were a household of four, my mother, my brother and sister, and I. My father had run off with his little wife, gone off and left us to die. We made a living, but just barely.

On another day, she told me the story of her brief career as a gum vendor. The following is a paraphrase from my field notes.

In those days, there were lots of soldiers around, so I sold gum. Where did I get the gum? I bought it in South Gate Market, of course.[12] My father had run away with his little wife and left us to starve; where were we going to get the money to eat and live? I sold gum to the soldiers and the "Western prostitutes" *(yang kalbo)*.[13] I didn't know the words and when they gave me American money, I didn't know what to do with it. After going around for a while, I learned what to say. Let's see if I can remember, "OK, *tankyu paeri mŭch'i.*" [A grin.] The soldiers would call after me, *"Saeksi, saeksi,"*[14] and grab at me, but I'd jerk away. One of the "Western misses" translated for me. This one guy said that he loved me and wanted to live with me. It went on for a while; I'd come to sell gum, and he'd be there saying "Babysan,[15] *present'o, present'o, chok'orat'o, chok'orat'o.* Come and live with me, Babysan." He'd grab at me, and I'd run away with my gum.

The man from the print company returned and asked me if I would come back to work. I knew that I'd make only a little bit of money that way, so I decided to keep on vending even though people said that the American soldiers would snatch away the young girls who sold gum. One day, this big black guy grabbed me and squeezed me. [She pantomimes a crushing embrace, eyes wide in remembered terror.] I ran all the way home, leaving the gum scattered on the ground. My mother went back later and picked it up. She told me, "Work for the print company, at least they're all Koreans there."

The taped narrative continues.

I went to work, and we were able to send my younger brother to school, to eat, and buy some clothes. I worked the night shift too. I was really too tired to do it, but I did it anyway and earned some more money. I worked like that day and night, and my face got pinched, like this [she sucks in her cheeks]. I couldn't even sleep; I had to earn money so we could live because my father had told us to drop dead and had run away with his little wife.

I got to be nineteen years old, and then I was so ill that everyone thought I would die, I mean it, I nearly died. I was still working in the print company and there wasn't any money for medicine. [But in another telling she says that she took both Western medicine from the pharmacy and Chinese herbal tonics and that nothing was effective. She probably means that there wasn't any money to spare, that her treatment was abbreviated.]

My head ached, my whole body ached. I was so ill that I wasn't able to eat anything—not that there was anything to eat. [Again, she blames her father for deserting the family.] My father's cousin told us to go and get a divination from a shaman. We did, and the shaman told us to have a *kut,* said that if we had the *kut* I would live. She was what they call an *anjŭn'gŏri mansin,* a seated shaman who chants over a drum and does not dance, the sort of *mansin* they have in Ch'ungch'ŏng Province. She was known as a great shaman. We didn't have much money then, so of course we only gave her a little.

When that shaman arrived for the *kut*, she asked me where I was hurting, but then she didn't hit the drum; she went to sleep! Everything was ready for the *kut*. Even though I was lying down sick, I really wanted her to hit that drum. "Come on, hurry up! Why are you sleeping? Hit the drum."

This is an early echo of the impatience she now experiences as a practicing shaman when a *kut* is slow to start. "Let's hit the drum and start dancing. Then we'll feel good." The drum sounds stir up the spirits and open the way to possession.[16]

"If that's the way you feel about it, I'll get started." I fell asleep as she was striking the drum. The *kut* went on all around me, and there I was, sound asleep. While I was asleep, a white-haired grandmother and grandfather arrived and started to massage me. They offered me some water from a dried gourd dipper. "Ahyu! What are you telling me to drink?"

"If you drink this, you'll survive." So I accepted the dipper, but just as I was about to gulp it down, some man tried to take it away from me. He was going to throw out the water, but the grandmother and grandfather shouted at him, "Stop that, you! This is for the child. Get out of here." So I drank down the water in a single gulp. I opened my eyes. Oh! They were having a *kut* and making a racket. It was all very strange. I told the shaman about my dream. "A grandfather gave me some water and told me to drink, so I drank it." "Well then, this means that you'll live. That was medicinal water *(yaksu)*, no doubt about it." She went on with the *kut*, and then that *mansin* asked me to become her spirit daughter *(sin ttal)*.

By "spirit daughter," do you mean that she wanted you to become a mansin?[17]

That's right. It was because I'd been ill for some time, and then when they'd held a *kut*, I'd gotten right up. But when the *mansin* said this, my mother shook and trembled and really carried on, "What do you mean 'spirit daughter'? Don't say such things in front of the child." My mother wouldn't agree to it, and was she ever worked up.

I recovered. But then I kept going up to the Immortal's Rock (Sŏn Pawi) on the hillside behind our house. My mother thought that I was acting strangely and wondered why I kept on going up there. She forbade it, but I felt drawn back and climbed up the hillside again. Since my illness had gone, I went back to work at the print shop. I went to work again, and I got sick again. I was sick, and I had to go to the outhouse. My mother told me to use the chamber pot but I refused; I didn't want to. Our house was on a steep hillside; we were here, and there was another house just below us. If people weren't careful, they could fall off our courtyard and land on our neighbor's roof. When I opened the gate that night, I don't know what happened, I blacked out completely and fell flat on the neighbor's roof, and then I fell off the roof. But I didn't have a single bruise on me. My mother carried me home on her back.

She paused here, for drama's sake, and then shifted her weight. The session was over, and she never again took up the thread of this story. On other occasions, she described frightening hallucinations recalled from the time of her illness. I remember vividly how she entertained a small cluster of neighbor women, her voice low with a hushed sense of mystery, "And then, I looked at my mother, and her face turned into the face of a tiger."

"What in the world! . . ."

"I had a little Buddha statue; my friend brought it from Japan, and I kept it on top of the dish cabinet. I saw flames burst out all around it. I'm telling you, the whole dish cabinet was in flames." In 1985 I asked her to tell me the story of the little Buddha statue, of which I had only heard bits and pieces. "You mean I've never told you that?"

It was when we were living in Seoul. In Korea in those days, the most highly prized fabric was imported satin. It was difficult to get ahold of, even if you had the money. Well, you know, my friend's husband was going to Japan and I gave him the money to buy me some. When I heard that he would be back within the next few days, I was so pleased. I waited for that cloth; I would make myself something pretty to wear. But he only brought cloth for his wife; he brought me that little tiny Buddha—the one that's in the shrine—and a red carrying cloth. "That's all you brought me? What do you mean by bringing me a toy?" He had thought that I would be so pleased with it, that I didn't really need the satin. Oh, I was angry! He told me to take some of the cloth that he had brought for his wife; we divided it up between us. I kept the Buddha. I set it out on top of the big desk I had in those days with two little dolls at its sides, turned ever so slightly askew.[18]

That night, just as I was going to sleep, as soon as I'd closed my eyes, a great ball of flame burst out of nowhere. The flames rose up, *ttuk, ttuk,*

ttuk, higher and higher. "Fire, fire!" I screamed for my mother. "Crazy girl, what fire?" She told me to turn on the light, and it was gone. Odd. Once again, I turned out the light to go to sleep, and there the ball of fire burst out again! It rose up above where I was sleeping, up where the Buddha was. My mother called me a "crazy girl" and said that she wouldn't have any more of it, this talk of flames rising up. She grabbed the Buddha and took it to the storage closet off the veranda.

I closed my eyes to go to sleep but then I heard *tchilluk, tchilluk, tchilluk,* and then *silluk, silluk, silluk,* the sound of the Buddha coming back into the room. I screamed for my mother to turn on the light. She slapped me, called me "crazy girl," and told me to turn the light on and see for myself. The Buddha hadn't come back in. But when I closed my eyes again, there it was, *tchilluk, tchilluk*. Now my mother went out and covered it up with a carrying cloth and asked why I was still making a fuss. No matter what she did, I kept waking up, no matter how hard I tried to go to sleep. No matter where the Buddha had gone, when I opened my eyes, there it was. I took it out of the storage cabinet and when I placed it on the desk again, it gave off a glow [she shapes an aura of light with her hands]. It was bright like a lamp.

My mother realized that this was nothing ordinary and went to a great *mansin,* one who was known in those days as Squatter Shack Mansin, and asked about it. "We received a Buddha, a little tiny Buddha. Now my daughter keeps insisting that it's surrounded by a ball of fire." The *mansin* said, "You absolutely must not get rid of it." We put up a shelf in our room and set it up there with a little water jar for my mother to keep filled with water, but she became neglectful. I was a maiden then, just a kid, what did I know?

How old were you then?

Sixteen, I think. That's right, because I was fifteen the year that the Korean War broke out. My mother found it bothersome to keep pouring and replacing the water so, by and by, she stopped doing it altogether, and by and by I got sick. I was so ill that I was on the brink of death; everyone said that I was going to die, but then if we had a *kut,* I would be fine. It was like that when I lived in my mother's house; I'd be so ill, but as soon as there was a *kut* I would get right up, no matter that I had been sick and dying.

Was this when you received the medicinal water in your dream?

[Prompted by my question, she tells, again, how the *mansin* arrived and went to sleep but was roused by the impatient girl, how she slept and was visited by a white-haired couple who gave her medicinal water from a gourd dipper, and how she was suddenly roused awake in the middle of the *kut*.] They were waking me up; they were going to exorcise me. I'd been startled awake and felt strange. In my dream the grandfather had been giving me water and now he wasn't there. "Where has the grandfather gone?" "So you've had a dream," the *mansin* said, "You'll live." And when they had done the *kut* and were leaving, I got right up and was well. I saw that grandfather exactly two times; I haven't seen him since.

Twice?

Right, twice. There was that time during the war when I was taken away by the People's Army. "Hey! It's getting late. You don't have much time." When he said that, I ran away and survived. [. . .] [She returns to the story of the little Buddha that intersects with the stories of her miraculous dreaming.]

I kept that Buddha with me while I was still in my mother's house. Then, when my sister was twenty-seven, she became a *mansin* and came back to stay with us [she was divorced]. She took it away.

What? She stole it?

She thought, why should we keep a Buddha in our house, in an ordinary house where people were living? Now that she was a shaman, she took it away somewhere and kept it. I didn't know what she had done with it. And once again, I became ill. I went up the mountain, to the rock shaped like a Buddha [she pantomimes the prayerful attitude of the stone configuration]. Every day, I went to the stream (to bathe), fixed rice, and went up there to make offerings.

How old were you then?

Sixteen, seventeen, I was sixteen years old.

You were sixteen when you had the kut?

Right. We did it when I was sixteen or seventeen and again when I was nineteen or so. My sister took the Buddha away. I was angry and sick to death. Now the *mansin* all said that I would have to get it back and set things right. But where should we look? You have to know where things are. My sister just said that she had given it away. I asked her coaxingly and she said that she had gone to Pure Hermitage Village, to the Maitreya Shrine (Mirŭk Tang). Nowadays it's not so far from Seoul, but back then there weren't any paved roads out here and no buses. You had to get off the bus at Righteous Town and walk in. [A sigh.] My mother and I went out there to make offerings, but to get to where the Buddha was, going all that way in my high-heeled shoes, my feet broke out in blisters and hurt. I went along in my bare feet, my stockings were all torn, but somehow we got there. The shrine keeper *(tangju)* was an old, bent grandmother who greeted us, "Oh, so you've arrived." My mother said, "We've come from Seoul." "Oh yes, the little Buddha's owner *(chuin)* has arrived." [She speaks in the whispering and portentous tones of the old shrine keeper.] "Oh no, we've simply come to prepare our rice and make our offerings to the Buddha." "Good. You can wash and cook your rice and take it up there." Oh, she was a bent-up old woman.

My mother washed our rice and vegetables in the clear water from a waterfall and prepared things just so. We went into the temple and made our offering, and then the grandmother gave us the little Buddha and told us to take it. "Why are you doing this, Grandmother? It belongs here. Why should we take it away?" "The Buddha says his owner has come, he's leaving." That's exactly what she said. So I brought the Buddha back and once again set it up in the room, just so. My mother offered clear water, but once again it was stolen. My sister stole it away again. Now it was really gone. I was nineteen years old when my sister took it away for good.

Did she really steal it twice? The sequence of events seems awkward but permits an interesting story about a visit to the Maitreya Shrine and a meeting with the bent old woman who knew the little Buddha statue's mind. Yongsu's Mother was again seriously ill in her early twenties, at the time of her daughter's birth, and once again after her marriage. Finally the gods descended and claimed her as a *mansin* while she danced at one of Chatterbox Mansin's *kut*. Her sister, already a *mansin*, took her around to *kut* as an apprentice.

From the time the gods descended, I was told to get back the Buddha. It had been so long, almost ten years. How would I know where to fetch it? But once I'd found it, they would give me visions and I would be able to do great invocations.

Who said?

The grandfather (unspecified god or gods). Somewhere I had to find it, but by then I had no idea where to look. I sat by myself. Since this was a grandfather who knew all about the matter, he ought to let me know if it's north or south or east or west, how many meters from here, if it's in a temple or a house in such and such neighborhood. So I sat there (hoping for inspiration). "You must go and get it back." "But I have to know where to look. Please show me." I sat. "Go and ask your teacher." [The word "teacher," *sŏnsaeng,* is strange in this context, perhaps chosen to again draw a parallel between her experiences as an apprentice *mansin,* my role as her student, and the larger world of learning.]

I went and asked my sister (since she was my "teacher"), but she said, "You think I know where it is? I have no idea." My little sister was there, so I asked her, "Do you know what became of your elder sister's little Buddha?" "I think she gave it away to a monk." That typhoid-taking thing! How was I going to find it if she'd gone and given it to some monk? The child had no idea. The grandfather had told me to look at my teacher's, but I came back empty handed. My head throbbed, my feet hurt, and I didn't have the slightest appetite. There was only the Buddha. I filled a little bowl with water and set it down. "I'll go and get it back if you just show me where it is." "Go and look at your teacher's, in the back." This was strange. I'd been told to ask there but my sister claimed that she didn't know anything about it. So early one morning I snuck over to have a look. They were eating breakfast inside, my mother, my elder sister, and my younger brother and sister. The shrine was in the back of the compound and I snuck in. [She pauses, for drama's sake.] There, I saw it!

It was there, but I couldn't steal it away in secret. After all, it was my sister's shrine. I went to someone else (another *mansin*) and asked. She said, "Buy rice, candles, and fruit and go make an offering, then bring it out with you." I took the candles and things and my sister said, "What's this all about?" "I've come to honor my Buddha." "And where is your Buddha?" "In your shrine, Sister." "It means nothing to me. You can take it or leave it."

Without even cooking the rice, I offered the uncooked grain and lighted the candles. I said, "Buddha mine, I'm going to take you with me,"[19] and fled back home with it. So once again it came back to me, the Buddha that I had received when I was fifteen years old [or sixteen or nineteen]. How many years is that? Fifteen, fifty-five, I'm fifty now, so that makes thirty-five years. It's come back to me, and I think that's how it was meant to be. The *mansin* were always going at it, zealously purging me, wielding their knives, really driving it out of me, but none of it worked, since I was always sickly. Now I know why.

She still has the little statue; it sits in her shrine, nestled on a tiny pillow beside the large gilt and plaster Buddha images. In 1985, when her business was prospering, she hired a master craftsman to cover the old pot metal with a layer of gilt.

Like the tale of her meeting with the Mountain God, the story of Changmi's illness evokes common themes in other shaman biographies. Divine beings often make dream visitations, usually bearing a bowl of medicinal water or a book of mystical teachings. Common, too, is the irresistible compulsion that draws the destined shaman to a temple, shrine, or sacred mountain.[20]

Like Yongsu's Mother, most shamans claim that they and their families resisted the calling. There are several reasons for this: the shaman's traditional lowly status, the disgrace of her public performance, and a pragmatic suspicion of charlatans who too willingly claim the voice of the gods to earn a livelihood (Harvey 1979, 1980; Kendall 1985:57–65; Choi n.d.:99–100). The mother's tantrum was a predictable response to the shaman's request for a spirit daughter. Given similar advice, the mother of Pyŏngyang Mansin, one of Harvey's informants, kept the information from her fourteen-year-old daughter for years after the *kut* that had cured her of a mysterious illness (Harvey 1979:98). Pyŏngyang Mansin also had a relatively easy experience as a god-descended shaman; like Yongsu's Mother, she was claimed by her spirits while dancing at a *kut* in a costume borrowed from a shaman *(mugam)*. I suspect that for both of these women, tales of early portents assume added significance, enhancing the legitimacy of an otherwise temperate descent of the gods.

Yongsu's Mother finds several threads of divine influence that run through her early life and bind her to her calling. There is, of course, the Mountain God who saved her life, first with a warning dream and again with a dipper of medicinal water. In the tale of the Buddha statue, the little grandmother who accompanies the Mountain God plays a walk-on part. In the story of her mother and the Buddhist Sage, a story that links the children's fate to the actions of pious women and to the spiritual force they accrue, the little grandmother of the dream comes forward.

They gave me water from the dipper and I drank it. Even in my dream, even as I was drinking, the grandmother took the gourd dipper and rubbed my stomach with it. Even in my dream, I thought that this was odd. "Ahyu, that hurts! Why are you rubbing me?" "I'm doing this so you won't be sore." But I kept shouting, "It hurts, it hurts! What do you mean by coming here and rubbing a maiden's belly, Grandmother, I don't want it!" And then the grandmother took me on her back and I woke up in the middle of the *kut.* They were jumping and carrying on, making a racket. [. . .] That shaman grandmother said, "It means you'll live; that was the Buddhist Sage Grandmother and Mountain God Grandfather." [. . .] I suppose that was when my mother woke up, realized that there was no use in denying it; there's something to superstition after all.

In addition to the Mountain God and the Buddhist Sage, there is her long connection to the little Buddha statue, a source of personal power. In her tales, Yongsu's Mother finds these figures at significant turnings, signs of a marked and legitimate calling, and she speaks of them with considerable dramatic flair, not just for the anthropologist's benefit, but also for her clients. But many other things have happened to her, some without obvious spiritual design save insofar as her rotten luck is another mark of the shaman's destiny. Yongsu's Mother has some relatively happy memories of her early adulthood.

I was at the print company for a long time and became skilled. Because they considered me a skilled worker, they gave me a little more money, they paid me well. Because I'd been there so long, I knew how to do everything—printing the lines on paper, binding notebooks. Once we beat a rival company by assembling some ten thousand notebooks in thirty days. The rival company couldn't meet that deadline; their people had even worked overtime, but not us. They gave me a lot of responsibility. When the boss left early, he'd hand me the key so I could lock up for him. The next morning people would be lined up outside the door, shivering in the cold, and there would be the boss, shivering in his taxi. I'd stride by them all and open up.

In her early twenties she had begun to enjoy a new life, a consequence of changed social conditions after the war and the fact that she remained single to support her family. One day, seemingly out of the blue, Yongsu's Mother asked me, "Isn't the jitterbug the liveliest American dance?"

Not anymore, but how did you know about it?

I went to dancing school and learned the tango, rhumba, and waltz. Then I went out to dance halls around Seoul, sometimes with a group of friends from the print factory, and sometimes with the dancing teacher. I learned all the dances faster than my friends, and I really loved to go dancing. I would work all day and then go to the dance halls at night. When I'd come in late, my mother would ask where I'd been and I'd just say that I'd been working the night shift.

Did you go dancing with your lover? (See chapter 6.)

Yes, but I didn't enjoy it because he couldn't dance, and would scowl when other people asked me. [She twists her face into the long grimace of her remembered companion.] While I was dancing other people would ask for my address and so forth; he would grill me when I got back to the table.

I was really slim then, and wore a long skirt cinched in at the waist. My waist was small to begin with, but when I wore a belt—I had a red one and a blue one—it looked even tinier than it was. When my girlfriends wore tight skirts, their stomachs would stick out, but mine was flat as a board. The dancing teacher would plead with me to eat just a little bit more rice. I wore my hair long then, either in two braids or bound with a black tie so that it hung down my back in a ponytail. I wore it that way until my sworn sister *(suyang ŏnni)* asked me to go to church with her on Sundays. When I sat there during the service, my head would start to ache because nothing held my interest; I would just drift away. This elder sister thought that if I cut my hair it might help (stop the headaches). I intended to cut only a little, in those days unmarried women didn't have short hair, but I took off too much and I've been wearing it short ever since.

Her boredom in the Christian church probably presaged more than a change of hairstyle. The phrase *"Na wa chaemi ŏpsŏtta,"* "It didn't have any interest for me," is ambiguous and could imply more than a young girl's impatience with the Sunday service. When a particular course of ritual activity fails to produce a desired result, this is *chaemi ŏptta,* "no interest"; one lacks the appropriate spiritual connection. Yongsu's Mother seems to suggest that because she was a destined shaman, the spirits made her thoughts wander and her head ache whenever she visited the Christian church.[21] Looking backward, the past is filled with portent, and a change of hairstyle foreshadows a shaman's destiny, but years would pass before Yongsu's Mother received the next clear indication of her fate. In the meantime much else would befall her.

Bit by bit, our situation got better; we could buy rice to eat and clothes to wear, and that was just great! Things were going well for us when the time came round for my junior grandfather's sixtieth birthday celebration, his *hwan'gap.*[22] I said, "Mother's going to that birthday celebration." I insisted on it. By working at night I was able to buy her a Korean-style jacket and skirt and get my little brother a suit of Western clothes. They went to the junior grandfather's birthday celebration and my father and his little wife were there too. My father said, "What are you doing here?" but my mother didn't say a word. My little brother had been so tiny when our father ran away, and now he was already a child in primary school. "Is that child Tong-gil?"

"Yes."

"Hey you, come here," but that kid didn't budge.

The little mother went to give her greeting and bow to the junior grandfather and grandmother, but they wouldn't let her do it; they wouldn't accept her bow because she was only a little wife. She fled without giving a greeting, but my father stayed behind, the father who hadn't seen us for six or was it seven years? Because I'd been working in a factory, we'd been able to repaper the walls and ceilings of our house with clean paper. I wore high-heeled shoes and a Western dress. I said, "Father, come see us someday." I said that even though during the war, when we had tried to flee, there was no end to our troubles, and when I was in primary school I had gone to school hungry . . . My father had been a terror; he'd say that a girl shouldn't study and he'd chase after me, brandishing a stick to beat me . . .

She abandons her tale of reunion and again recapitulates the tale of her early life, how she snuck off to school in her bare feet, how her father threatened to beat her to death, and how the teacher came to the house to beg her parents to send her to school. But on another occasion, she took up the story of this day of revenge, a revenge which would ultimately prove to be expensive.

My father ran away with his little wife and six years passed; we assumed he'd gone off and died somewhere. It was the sixtieth birthday of our grandfather's younger brother (our junior grandfather), and my mother went to that celebration wearing two rings on her finger and a big, thick sweater that I'd knit for her. It had been years since Father and the little mother ran away with the barley. For all he knew, we'd starved to death. But there was Mother with rings on her finger and a nice, big sweater. The little mother didn't have a sweater or a ring. My father asked my mother, "How did you get here?"

"What do you mean 'How did you get here?' We walked of course."

[And she tells again how her little brother did not recognize his long-absent father and stubbornly refused to greet him.]

The little mother was there too, but when she went to bow to the junior grandfather he said, "I don't want it. I won't accept it," and turned away. [. . .] So she turned to the junior grandmother, but she also refused to accept the little mother's bow. The little mother went up and tried to bow again, but once again the junior grandmother and grandfather refused her. Well, the little mother was really ashamed; she didn't know what to do, so she ran away home. My mother asked, "Where did she go?"

My father just said, "She left."

"Why did she go?"

"They wouldn't accept her greeting, so what was the point of staying? She left." Mother wondered whether she should go or stay.

Because she had sold water (from house to house) and I'd worked in a factory, she was able to go to the *hwan'gap* in nice clothes and wearing the gold rings that I had bought for her. My father thought that we must be really rich, so he came to borrow money. If we'd had our own best interests at heart, we would have told him to drop dead, right? He left after two days, but then, one month later, he was back again asking for money. Mother, just like a fool, gave him money again. He took it and left, and then when the money was spent, he came back again. The neighbors all told her, "You're crazy. Why give him money? Your husband told you to drop dead, cast you out, ran away. And after all that, you give him money?" The neighbors told me [in a throaty whisper], "You know, your mother's giving your father money. Make her stop."

"Mother, did you give Father money?"

"Yes." [A small, shamed voice.]

The next time he came, we didn't give him any money. As he was leaving, he said, "If that's the way it is, don't have anything more to do with me, even if I'm dying," and he went away. Even our paternal aunt (our father's sister) had told us, "Your father is farming and makes a good living." But then he got sick and his belly swelled up. He said that he was going to the hospital and we asked him if he had the money for it. He said no, that he'd come expecting it from us. He went to Severance Hospital, but they couldn't do anything for him; then he went to another hospital in West Gate. He could only eat the most expensive foods like beef, crayfish, sea bream, and fruits like bananas and oranges at five hundred won apiece. [This was a plausible price for an imported banana in 1977.] He was with us for thirteen days and that cost us sixty thousand won. He had told us to die, and had never so much as given me a set of clothes or a pair of shoes. I said to him, "When you were young and strong, you took the little mother and lived it up with her, but you told us to drop dead. Now that you're sick, you've come back and used up all our money."

The little mother came for him and said she was going to a *mansin* for a divination. We'd done it already, but the *mansin* had told us he was going to die. The little mother wouldn't accept this. She said that there should be a *kut.* She didn't have anything to wear, so she borrowed the jacket and skirt I was wearing and went out to a *mansin*. This *mansin* said that he didn't have to die and set a date for a *kut.* My mother went down to the country (where my father had been living) for the *kut.* She'd contributed some money, but the little mother hadn't spent any of it to buy rice cake or fruit or any of the other things that you need for a *kut.* And then during the *kut* the *mansin* just kept asking my mother for cash, and my mother had to keep digging into her pockets. That *mansin* didn't get so much as ten won from the little mother. It was the little mother who'd told the *mansin* to keep after Mother like that. When Mother came back, I asked her how it had gone, and she groaned and said that it looked as though he was going to die anyway. That was in the first month of the year, and in the second, we got the death announcement. Since we didn't have any more money, we sent food—soy sauce, sesame oil, red pepper—we took all the provisions we had in the house and sent them to the country. Still they criticized us for not spending money, even though they could use this stuff when they fixed food for all the guests, couldn't they?

SIX

The Reluctant Bride

I went out to work and came back home, and so it went. And then one day, as I was on my way home from work, just when I'd nearly reached the house, a man planted himself in my path, right smack in front of me. He just stood there. Of course he wanted to force me to say something, but I just pretended that I didn't know what he was after and went on my way. When I went out to work the next morning, the man was standing there, right smack in my path again. If my father knew about it, he'd kill me. I mean he'd kill me if he saw me talking with a man, so I couldn't say a thing. But when I came out from work in the evening, there was that man again!

Things went on like this for a while until one day the rain poured down. And didn't that man bring two umbrellas? He gave me one and told me to use it. I brought it back the next day, said that it had served me well, and went on my way to work. Things went on like this for about a month. Naturally enough, we began to strike up conversations. That's how it happened. Eventually he took me to the movies, we talked, we began to keep company, and then one day my father found me out.

When my father knew about it, he whipped me. He said he'd kill me for running around with a man. I told him I wouldn't do it again, I begged him, I told him I was sorry. He whipped me some more. The next morning, when I went out to work, that fellow was standing there again, but this time I just went to work without saying a word. He came running after me shouting, "*Misu* Pak, *Misu* Pak, when can I see you?" I told him that my father had whipped me and that he must not come again. I told him to go away, to leave me alone so that my father wouldn't beat me. Time passed, two months, three months, a whole year. That fellow was always running after me. My father forbade me to go to work because I always saw that man on the way.

So I couldn't even work. I had to stay home doing nothing. The boss came over and asked me why I wasn't working, and I told him that my father would beat me.

The incident becomes a replay of her early life. The ogre father bars Changmi from work that she did well, work that gave her much satisfaction, just as he had prevented her from attending school. The boss comes by to find out why a favored worker is slacking off, just as the conscientious teacher had sought her out a decade earlier. The parallels are so tidy as to be suspicious, particularly since the father's intervention belies a salient theme of her early life, her father's abandonment and disappearance. He simply should not have been there. I wondered if the wrathful, punishing father was a projection, even in retrospect, of her own guilt and uncertainty at new emotions and an increasingly dangerous flirtation, a consequence of both the changing times and the disconnected circumstances of her own household. When I asked her in 1985 about her father's beatings she said, "Oh no, my father wasn't there. My father never saw that man's face." She took up the thread of this tale on another day.

You know my daughter who lives in Willow Market? Her surname is Pak (like mine). I originally thought that I would marry that man, but I didn't marry him after all. He was fond of me, and my older sister urged me to marry him. How did I meet him? Well, he chased after me. He'd stand there when I came out of the factory.

Oh, you mean that man, the one who brought you an umbrella on a rainy day?

Yes, that's the one. When I look back on it, I really did intend to marry that man. We'd dated and even promised each other that we would marry. I'd asked him, "Are your mother and father still alive?" He'd told me they were and that he also had a sister and an elder brother. I said, "Well then, let's go and pay our respects to your mother and father."[1] Good grief (I was naive)! "We'll go later on," he said. This was a bit odd, but then one day he did take me to meet his sister. She was older than I thought she would be, with a lot of children. "What about your elder brother?"

"He lives far away." That was that.

Well, we dated. For three, then four years, we'd gone around together. So then, well, didn't I find myself growing fonder of him? Things went on like this, and my girl child was conceived. I was carrying a baby in my belly, so naturally I thought, "We should get married before my belly swells." But when the man saw things turn out this way, he began to fight with me; he despised me. I wondered, "Why is he treating me this way? Could it be that he's found another lover? Why should he suddenly turn on me?"

A close friend of mine stopped by, "So you're here all alone. Let's go somewhere."

"We've gone around together (for so long). Why should he suddenly despise me?" My friend said, "Let's go for a divination," and I went out with her to have my fortune told. This is what the diviner said, "It's the baby that's set its mother and father at odds. Abort the baby."[2]

"How can I abort this baby? I can't do it."

"Only if you abort this baby will be you able to live with your husband. If you don't do it, you won't have a life together." If I wanted to stay with him, I would have to destroy the baby. I went home and talked it over with my mother. She said, "Crazy woman! How do you think you can get rid of this baby?" She was ferocious. I went to get that man, but they said he was at work. I went out to meet him and said my piece, "Since this baby's come between us, it's impossible for us to love each other. We should destroy this baby."

Now he was furious, "How dare you say you're going to get rid of this baby? Destroy this baby and I'll kill you. I won't have it. You can't do it." That's how much that man despised me. I brooded over how his feelings for me had changed once I became pregnant.

Then one day my elder sister came for a visit and that man happened to stop by the house while she was there. My sister started questioning him. "What do your parents do? What does your elder brother do for a living?" He wasn't able to answer her. "Where does your mother live? Where does your elder brother live? If you don't tell us these things, then how can you expect to marry? We have to meet your parents. Bring them over to the house." But days passed, and that man didn't bring his parents over.

Belatedly, the meddlesome elder sister assumed the role of the absent father, attempting to protect the interests of pregnant Chang-mi. Claimed by her spirits as a destined *mansin,* the sister had disappeared into the countryside and become the spirit daughter of Boil Face Mansin. Reunited with her family after three years, she assumed an increasingly significant role in their lives. Yongsu's Mother's story continues.

I loathed him to death, but what could I do? I was carrying his child, so I would have to marry him, wouldn't I? There was nothing I could do about it. But I wanted to see if he'd been deceiving me. I went to investigate.

Where?

To his sister's house and then to the neighborhood where he said his brother lived. When I asked, his sister told me that their parents had died when they were all children. They were dead; they didn't exist. Well then, how had this man been raised? She told me that she had raised him herself. Then I went and sought out his elder brother. He was living in a tiny rented room; he took room and board there, he had never married. Now wasn't I just devastated! Here was this man who was always so well turned out, always with his clothes just so and wearing a necktie, but when you saw his family, they didn't have anything to speak of. His brother may as well have been a beggar, wearing some old pajamas. Oh, I was disappointed!

That night, the man came to my house, and then didn't we quarrel. "Why did you lie to me? You said your mother and father were alive, but they aren't. Even your elder brother is just living in a little rented room. Your sister doesn't have it easy. Why did you deceive me?" Only then did he tell me the truth. When his brother was nine years old and he was six years old, his parents died. He said that his brother had never married but, as the eldest son, he had been given their mother's house. Even so, the brother was worthless and sold the house to feed his appetite for drink.

"I won't marry you. I'm going to abort the baby."

Hadn't you already said that you were going to abort?

Yes, but he wouldn't let me. That's why I went to his family, to tell them that we were going to get married, but then I saw that they had nothing, not even a rice bowl. Where would we live? I told him, "I'm not going to marry you."

"If you won't marry me, then let's die."

"How do you expect me to marry you, you worthless bastard? You don't have a father or a mother. Your brother's no better than a beggar. If I married you, where would you take me to live?"

As for the baby, one month passed, then two, and then eight months, nine months. I tied a cloth girdle around my stomach with a string because my stomach was sticking out. I'm tall and I've always been skinny; even when I was carrying a baby, I didn't show a big belly. My mother said, "You shouldn't go outside when you're this far along." "My belly isn't big." Even so, I was embarrassed and bound it in.

What did people do in those days if they wanted an abortion? Did they take

Chinese medicine? [I wanted to probe for the options that might have been available to an unmarried but pregnant young woman.]

No, they went to hospitals. [Thus distracted, but not really interested in this line of inquiry, she told me the story of the reunion with her runaway father at the junior grandfather's *hwan'gap* and of her father's subsequent opportunism. This was a necessary, if awkwardly sequenced, foreshadowing of events that would transpire at the time of his death. She caught up the thread of her story.]

This wretched excuse of a bridegroom of mine would raise a fuss whenever he saw me because I refused to marry him. The ten months[3] had passed and the baby'd been born, a girl. When that man came over, I didn't have the least bit of strength left. I was sitting on the veranda. I told him, "Take this baby and go. It's your daughter, so take her away. I can't marry you. You're impossible. You don't have anywhere to take it, do you? I'm supposed to raise it in my mother's house. Bastard, how am I going to live, with no money for the child?"

He'd been drinking all day. He said, "You'll die and then I'll die." He was going to beat me to death. I'd never seen anything like it in all my life. He slapped my face and beat me. But you can bet that I stood up to him and yelled back, "What do you mean by beating me?"

"Why won't you marry me?"

"You're worthless. I can't do it. Take your bastard and go. I'm going to live alone." I raised such a racket that he nearly killed me. He grabbed me and kicked me with a shod foot. He kept it up and, well, how much strength does a woman have? I lost consciousness. After a while I woke up and found myself in the hospital. It was strange to be there. Had I gotten there all by myself? Even today I have a scar over my rib cage where he had kicked me so hard that I'd fainted dead away. There I was, in the hospital and in pain, and this bastard came right into the room. I started to scream and threw my pillow at him, "Get out of here you bastard! You tried to kill me! Get out of here!" The doctor told me that I shouldn't move. That day all I could do was use my mouth and yell. I left the hospital a week later, went home, but no sooner did I arrive than there he was, threatening me with a stick or a hammer or something like that. This guy was so frightening that I couldn't even live at home.

It happened that my child had been born on the sixth day of the second month and then we got the announcement that my father had died on the seventeenth, at the little mother's house. We were supposed to go down there for the funeral, but since I had just given birth, I wasn't able to go.

Even though I stayed at home, I loosened my hair, put on white clothes, filled a small earthen jar with water, spread a mat in the courtyard, and bowing to the east, west, south, and north, I cried out the mourner's lament. Mother had gone to Father's funeral and I was carrying on like this when that bastard came again, all fitted out with a laundry paddle. "So you're mourning. Well then, you'll die and I'll die."

"Who do you think you're going to kill, you wretch? Bastard! Why don't you just get lost?" All of the uncles from the neighboring houses (supported me and) said things like, "Look here, if you want to beat someone up, how about trying to kill me?" He refused. I can't tell you how exasperating it was to have him always chasing after me like that. After the funeral my mother returned. My mother had continued on in the place where she had lived with her husband, but now that she had been to his funeral, she knew that he was gone for good. She began to say things like, "If I live in Seoul, I'll just be cremated and cast away. I don't want that to happen. I'd rather go back to my old village so that when I die, I'll be buried in a proper grave on a mountainside."

"Mother, where is your village?"

"In Clear Spring District."

"Do you think that I know where Clear Spring District is?"

"Willow Market."

Now how would I know where that was? I'd been born and raised in Seoul, so I had absolutely no idea. By then [as a consequence of marriage and divorce], my sister was living in Bright County and she knew that area well. Mother kept on, "I want to go back to my village, to live and die there. Let's move." So without letting that person know, we quickly sold our house in Seoul and, just like that, we moved down here.

Even now, Yongsu's Mother considers herself a citizen of Seoul and more sophisticated than her country neighbors. Whether she blames her sister's urging or her mother's sentimentality or her own brutal lover, she bitterly regrets the move down to the country and the match that was made for her there. Her mother's anxieties about cremation were current in the summer of 1977 when her son, Tong-gil, and his wife contemplated a move back to Seoul. While dancing at a *kut,* the old woman was possessed again by her powerful Body-Governing God and cried out, "I won't go, I won't go, that's all there is to it. This is my native place. The weather's fine, the scenery's fine. Why should I go anywhere else?"

In Changmi's obstinate refusal to marry, I thought that the lady did protest too much. Was the prospect of marrying a penniless orphan any worse than her eventual marriage to a penniless widower? I assumed that I must be naive concerning the depth of Korean prejudices, but I was suspicious. Once, when we were discussing a foundling child who had been left at the mill, she whispered with gossipy detachment, "It's the child of an unmarried woman, some maiden's child." I asked her why, when abortions were so easily available in Korea, an unmarried woman would carry her pregnancy to term. "They think that the man will come around once the baby is born," she said, again with perfect detachment, and I wondered. But in 1985 she told me yet another version of the events that prompted her household to move to the country. In the story of the little Buddha statue, she described her illness after the Willow Market Daughter's birth as one in the series of afflictions that beset her before she became a *mansin* and was reunited with her Buddha. She had mentioned this illness before in an abbreviated, if dramatic, account, told out of context when I had asked about postpartum behavior and breast-feeding in my initial standard interview. Now she set these events into a larger narrative frame.

I was so ill that everyone said I was dying. My mother felt that if it had to be, so be it, but that I ought to at least see my close kin again before I died. She summoned my sister, fast. My sister called in this doctor and that doctor and called them all back again, but my condition just went from bad to worse.

Where did it hurt?

My stomach was so sore and I was all twisted and wrenched. I couldn't breathe for thrashing back and forth. One person said that it was appendicitis and another said, well, that it was difficult to say just what my illness was. They all said different things. My sister said, "Ai, things don't look good for this child. Let's give her an outing."

Outing?

Right. "This child, living in Seoul, should be able to enjoy the fresh air at least once (before she dies)." She brought me to Boil Face Mansin. Since I seemed to be on the brink of death, my mother was opposed to it. "If she has to die, let her at least die at home. Leave her be. What do you mean by carrying off the dying?" She was afraid that I would die away from home and become a wandering ghost *(kaeksa)*, but my sister was stubborn and took me along with her. Boil Face Mansin's brother-in-law ran a clinic for Chinese medicine. He looked me over and gave me two packets. I took them right away, and then I thought I'd die, the pain was so bad. He ran back, read my pulse, and gave me pills, not Chinese medicine. I was a little better, so I kept on taking that medicine for forty, maybe fifty days. I lived! My mother sent my brother with fish and seaweed for me and rubber shoes that she'd bought. By and by, I recovered from my illness. It took a year, I was there for a year with Boil Face. My illness disappeared and then, bit by bit, I recovered my strength, although I was too weak to wander very far. I would just sit and watch the people going back and forth with A-frames on their backs. In the fall I was a little better and caught grasshoppers. Then I said that I was going up to Seoul. My sister said, "Why go? I'll go up to Seoul." She went and arranged for my mother to move and brought her back down here. [In 1985 she chuckled at the remembered surprise, her old anger gone.] We lived here for a year, two years passed, and then I got married.

[I questioned her further on the particulars of her illness.]

I gave birth to my daughter and then almost immediately I was in pain.

Almost immediately, your appendix?

Not my appendix. They said it was my appendix, but it was really ghost play *(kwisin norŭm).*

And then your daughter's father went into the hospital and tried to kill you and . . .

Oh no. Since I had become ill immediately after giving birth, when they took me to the hospital for an appendectomy they said that they couldn't operate on a new mother. Another doctor was called and he said that it wasn't my appendix. The bad blood in my belly hadn't come out; it had formed a lump like this. [She makes a solid fist.] So they took me back to the hospital and I had an injection and took some medicine. I even took Chinese medicine, but I didn't get any better. Then my sister took me to Boil Face.

Did you have a kut *before you left? In Seoul?*

We were going to have one but then my sister heard all the neighbors say that I was dying. She thought that she would take me on an outing and then, if I lived, she would do a *kut* for me. If it looks as though someone is going to die, you don't do a *kut;* you just pray and so forth *(chisŏng tŭrida).* Boil Face—she was a great *mansin*—Boil Face came and did an exorcism *(p'udakkŏri).*[4]

But what about your daughter's father, your lover? How did you separate?

Well, that, it just happened. It was a time of great turmoil.[5] I don't know what became of him.

You got pregnant and then you separated?

Yes. But in those days they were all going into the army. Besides, that man didn't have a mother or a father. He had an elder sister, so I went to her, but even she didn't know where he'd gone.

Did that man know that you were pregnant?

Oh he knew, all right, he knew. And I have no idea where he went.

This second version accords more neatly with my own sense of human foibles, and I am inclined to accept the logic of these events. The earlier version might have salved her pride, a pride still evident in 1985—"after all, that man didn't have a mother or a father"—while transforming the author of her disappointment into an object of rage. Objectively, of course, I do not know that the tale told in 1985 is necessarily more true than the tale told in 1977 or that the emotions mustered when she describes her homicidal lover, punishing father, or red informer are any less real in the telling.

The earlier text continues.

My baby was just a little thing when we moved to Willow Market. Once she had passed her first birthday, my elder sister said to me, "You should get married." "I won't. I'd rather die than marry. Keep the baby here, and I'll provide for her. I can't go on living in the country; I'm going back to my job in Seoul. It'll be a long time before I get married."

"If you go back to Seoul, that man will catch you and kill you."

"Kill me? I don't think so. I'll keep myself hidden. Why should he catch me?"

"If he so much as catches a glimpse of you, he'll be after you."

I had cousins and uncles who could hide me. That bastard had no idea that I'd left Seoul for the countryside. He thought that I was somewhere in Seoul and had gone looking for me there. My child was barely into her second year. I said, "I'm absolutely not going to get married. You can bet your life on it." And the man they wanted me to marry was so old, he looked about forty.

[And now she begins the story that I had heard before.] It was the tenth month, and market day. I was wearing a red skirt and a lovely jacket with blue cuffs [or a yellow jacket and a pink skirt]. I told my mother that I was going to the market. She said that she was steaming beans for soy sauce and asked me to light the fire. I said, "I'll come right back from the market and light the fire for you then." I was about to go out when a man and a woman came in and asked for my sister. My sister's house was right next to ours so I yelled over, "Sister, you've got guests." She ushered them into the room to talk.

"Hey, come here."

"What do you want?"

She opened the door and looked at me, "Go and order a bowl of noodles."

"Sure."

She closed the door. I ordered the noodles, set them on a tray, and brought them in. I didn't know that the guests had come to look me over. As I set down the tray, the man kept staring at me.

"Mother, I'm going to the market."

"Light the fire first."

"All right."

"Fetch the tray."

I opened the door and went in for the tray, but he'd eaten only a mouthful. They were all laughing and talking away. I was lighting the fire in the flue when the guests came out, the man and the woman together. The man left, but the woman came around back and said, "I want to have a word with you."

"What do you mean?"

"That man came to have a first meeting with you."[6]

"It's no concern of mine that he came for a first meeting. I'm not going to get married. What do you mean by coming to look me over?" She told me that the man was waiting just outside. There wasn't anything I could do short of bolting myself inside the house.

"Just say the word. Just say 'OK' or 'No.' " [For our mutual amusement, she uses English words.]

"I won't get married. I won't go. Why do you want to marry me off to an old guy like that?" What could I do? The man was out there waiting. "Get out! What do you mean by looking me over without asking me first?"

So that person (the matchmaker) went back into my sister's room. My elder sister had arranged this secret first meeting without consulting me. They called Mother back in again, and now Mother was urging me to marry. "I can't go through with it. If one wants to marry, then one marries, but if one doesn't, one doesn't. Isn't that the way it should be?[7] Besides, I don't want to marry that man, he's too old."

Now my sister started screaming and pounding on the veranda. "You're killing me! Why won't you marry, you slut!" I realized that they had resolved to do this to me because I was living off the charity of my own family. It didn't matter that she was my own sister (she still begrudged me food).

"Do you despise me so much that you have to send me away? If you want to get rid of me, there's nothing I can do." Then I howled and shook. "Do what you want, I don't care!"

"Then it's settled," (the matchmaker said).

"What's settled?"

"You know what I mean."

"Get out of here!"

"Don't say such things."

The matchmaker left and I stood there bawling.

"Why won't you get married? Is this something to fight about?"

"How can I marry that old guy?"

My sister said, "Your horoscope is bad; you have to marry an older man to make things right."

"I don't want to."

My sister kept on insisting. "Do it, do it."

"All right then, go and investigate the other side, see how he's living."[8]

"I'll take care of that, don't you worry. The matchmaker is faultless."

When I thought of going away and leaving my baby in my sister's care, I was overwhelmed with sorrow, and my tears gushed. I cried unstintingly. But four days later, that man came back. He came and went without even seeing me; I hid in the outhouse. They called me, but after a while, he left. Then I came out of the outhouse.

"Where were you?"

"In there."

"You know, that man was here but you missed him."

"What's it to me?"

The next day was market day. My sister gave me some money and said, "Go and buy yourself some makeup."

"No, thanks. Why would I want to make myself up?"

"Buy what you like. Here's the money."

"Money? When did I ask for money?"

"Why are you behaving this way? Let's get going."

"What's the point?"

"You might see something that you'll want to buy."

"I don't want a thing." That man had left some money with her for my preparations. I didn't want his money, I was putting my foot down, but she kept insisting.

"What's there to buy, anyway?"

"Have your hair cut. Get a permanent. How about it?"

Now I got mad. I turned away from her and went back into the house.

Once inside, I cried, "That slut! Why does she want to go and marry me off behind my back?" I went to my mother and howled, "Does she so begrudge me my food that she has to chase me out? If the two of you actually do this to me, then once I'm married, I'll never come back home, not once my whole life long."

Since she was set on getting rid of me, my sister said, "This isn't an auspicious year for her to get married, so we'll marry her in the long moon month" [considered the end of the year and a neutral time]. There, with her own lips she had said that it was ill-fated, even as she hastened to send me off. That was how much she begrudged me my food. Oh, I was miserable! We passed a big river on the way to my husband's house and I thought, "I should just throw myself in there and die."

The wedding was on the eighteenth day of the long moon month. That man arrived. I'd cut my hair and had a permanent. How could I avoid it? It wasn't as though I wanted to get married, I certainly didn't. My sister had ordered me to get married, so there was nothing I could do but go through with it. They held a feast and we departed. I cried my heart out in the bus, smearing my face with tears. Oh how I cried, *"Uyi, uyi."* I'd made up my face but that was all smeared away.

"Shall I wipe your face with my handkerchief?" He was offering to wipe my face. He wanted me to stop crying. I told him, "I didn't want to get married. I'd intended to go back to my job in Seoul and then, when I'd earned a lot of money, I'd get married. My sister forced me into this."

"I'll take care of you. Don't cry." [She is more sympathetic to her husband here than in the tale told in chapter 2.]

On the journey to my husband's house, we came to the wide Imjin River. If you had a pass they would let you across, but you couldn't cross if you didn't have one. I was a bride on my way to my husband's house so, of course, I didn't have a pass. The long bridge stretched out in front of us. They made you get out at the bridge to be cleared by the antiespionage unit, then they gave you permission to proceed. They said that I needed a pass to get through, so my children's father had to go into the office to straighten things out while I waited outside. [For the first time, she uses the intimate phrase, "my children's father," instead of calling her husband "that man."] The men who were working on the bridge started to talk about me, "She's so thin, too skinny. How's a bride like that going to manage up here?" They even threw stones at me, but I didn't so much as let on that I was aware of them. Standing there by the river, my feet were so cold that I could die, and my so-called bridegroom didn't emerge for the longest time.

One of the men threw a stone that landed square on my foot and did that hurt! ["You bet it hurt!" she said in 1985, listening to this section of my old tape recording. "Making trouble for a new bride." She gave a contemptuous sniff, then smiled.] Then my children's father came back out and asked for my citizen's registration card. I opened my bag and drew it out, obediently, without a word. [She contradicts the obstinacy of her earlier story, the show of defiance that was, perhaps, wishful thinking. She elaborates, probably in response to my quizzical expression.] The card gives your name and address and everyone but the reds (North Korean spies) has one, so if you were stubborn about showing it, you got into a lot of trouble. That's why everyone just showed their cards.

The ferry crossed over to the other side of the river. My husband put out his hand to help me down. Just as the boat landed, someone rode up on a bicycle and greeted my children's father. Yongsu's Father looked just like that man on the bicycle. I remarked on it but he said that it was just some distant relation. He lied. I thought that I saw a close resemblance between the two men. On the other side there was another check point. We paused there (for clearance) and went on. There weren't any taxis, there weren't any buses, there wasn't anything over there. From that point on, we walked, oh how we walked. My feet were popping with blisters. I asked where the house was, and he said that it was right ahead. His younger brother had gone on ahead, racing along on his bicycle. I saw a big girl toss out some water and go back into one of the houses. That was the very house. I got a good look at it, a straw-roofed house leaning askew, just like a beggar's hovel. I stood outside the main gate and stared at it, wondering how I could spend even a day living there like a beggar.

We went inside. The main room was tiny, with a single cabinet, nothing else. There was a second room, too. I went inside and they brought in some food. They didn't even have rice bowls; they'd piled up the rice in soup bowls, crockery bowls [not brass or stainless steel].

Once, but only once, she told me that she felt responsible for her husband's death. Had she been cognizant of her destiny, heeded the signs, then perhaps he would not have died. The thought had struck her as she sat alone in her house, brooding over the past. This is a paraphrase from my field notes:

On my wedding day there were many guests and they'd feasted until late at night. They (the married women) were keeping watch on the nuptial chamber while I sat there scowling.[9] My sister-in-law was exhausted and fell asleep in the second room. She dreamed that I was right there in the room with her, sitting on the floor and hitting an hour-glass drum. All of the grandfathers' costumes were strung on a line over my head, the way we fix them during a *kut*. I should have known then.

My husband and I fought constantly after we were married, and then he got sick and died. When he was ill, I went to a *mansin* but she said that he would probably die. She told me to make an offering in the shrine, but I didn't know what to do. My sister-in-law went with me so that she could show me. I was supposed to raise my arms over my head and bow, but my arms stuck fast to my sides; I couldn't budge them. The grandfathers were telling me that I was going to become a *mansin*, that my husband would die, that it was useless to make offerings in the shrine on his behalf. He died and on the second anniversary of his death, we had the great send-off ending the mourning period *(taesang)*, and then the first anniversary after the mourning period *(ch'ŏtki)*. That was in the fourth month. When it was over, I went back to live in Willow Market, and in the seventh month I became a god-descended person.

She considers her swift possession, once she had completed the mourning period, fulfilled her obligations, and was no longer ritually polluted, to be another sign of the certainty of her calling. The years immediately after her husband's death were perhaps the bleakest of her life. She once described herself sitting behind closed doors of an evening, drinking with tears in her eyes. To support her three children, she peddled, "I sold clothing, I sold fish, I even sold little dried shrimp. I went around with all those things." When business was good she thought, "Now things will work out for me." Then she began to slowly lose her capital, to suffer once again from the ill fate that marked her as a destined shaman. Elsewhere I have recorded the story of her divine possession, how she went to one of Chatterbox Mansin's *kut* and Chatterbox Mansin told her to use the *mugam*,[10] to dance to a mild euphoria in one of the shaman's costumes, the Mountain God's robe.

I said, "What do you mean use the *mugam?* It's shameful for me to dance like that." But the Chatterbox Mansin kept saying, "It'll give you luck. You'll be lucky if you dance." So I put on the clothes and right away began to dance wildly. I ran into the shrine, still dancing, and grabbed

> the Spirit Warrior's flags. I started shouting, "I'm the Spirit Warrior of the Five Directions," and demanded money. All of the women gave me money. I ran all the way home. My heart was thumping wildly. I just wanted to die like a crazy woman. We talked about it this way and that way and decided there was no way out. So the next year I was initiated as a *mansin*. (Kendall 1985:59)

We had reached the end of our summer sessions. She had already told me the tales that were most important to her, the life that she had wanted me to hear. By mid-July her youngest stepdaughter had returned home, announcing that she was ready to marry. She had quit her factory job after raising a substantial sum of money for her dowry. Now Yongsu's Mother was busy again, complaining at the expense and bother of marrying off a daughter, but clearly enjoying herself. Our hours of uninterrupted conversation were suspended until the late fall. There was an engagement party to organize, a wedding feast, and countless purchases to be made: gifts of clothing, a watch, and a ring for the groom; gifts for the members of his immediate family, furniture, bedding, cooking equipment, a blender, and a television set. Each time I visited, Yongsu's Mother would report on the results of the latest shopping expedition, proudly exhibiting the silk slippers that her stepdaughter would wear with her pink satin Korean dress at the engagement party, or the bathrobe they had just purchased for the groom. She called her daughter "robber woman" *(todungnyŏ)*, but she said it with a smile. She was making a good show, doing well by her stepdaughter, and was quite proud of herself.

I have presented Yongsu's Mother's life in near chronological order while suggesting the episodic and meandering sequence of our sessions and the repetition of significant themes. The organization of these four chapters nearly replicates the predetermined and linear structure of most ethno-biographies and, as such, is an appropriate response to the autobiographical task that Yongsu's Mother initiated between us. I have suggested throughout some ways in which the tales that I heard were already polished, but not frozen entertainments. I have underscored the points where dreams, portents, and more general bad luck help legitimize Yongsu's Mother's claim to the shaman profession.

While special to me (and to Yongsu's Mother), our relationship had numerous parallels in the work of other anthropologists and articulate informants. The story of our collaboration merely replicates a genre of life writing.[11] The conventions of this genre necessarily overlook the more ordinary circumstances in which Yongsu's Mother tells and polishes her tales among women who do not bear notebooks and tape recorders. This is the task of the remaining chapter, to show Yongsu's Mother invoking her tales, invoking as both incantation and justification, in circumstances not necessarily marked by the presence of an anthropologist.

SEVEN

Old Ghosts and Ungrateful Children

> A dream cannot be truly interpreted . . . unless it is attached to the dreamer, although it may be a pretty story and have distinct meanings for someone to whom it is narrated.
>
> —Leon Edel, *Literary Biography*

It was the tenth lunar month, November by the Western calendar. The harvest had been gathered in, the farmer could rest, it was again the *mansin*'s busy season. Clients would come to the *mansin*'s inner rooms, sit on the hot floor, and receive divinations; some clients would sponsor *kut,* and some would call the *mansin* to sing *kosa* invocations when the family honored the household gods with rice cake offerings made of the newly harvested grain.[1] But Yongsu's Mother sat at home; business was off. No one called her to preside at their *kosa,* no one tapped on the door seeking a divination, and three regular customers cancelled scheduled *kut,* even after she had pulled out her charts and found them lucky days to match their horoscopes. She heard roundabout that one of these women had held her *kut* with another *mansin.* A year ago, Yongsu's Mother had spent the entire tenth month going hither and yon to *kosa* and *kut,* and just last month she had been busy. Her present inactivity was strange, ominous, and Yongsu's Mother was worried. "My fortune is blocked" *(uni maegyŏtta).* She was brooding and sleeping badly.

When she thought about it, her luck had not been good since her stepdaughter's wedding, not since she had given *yŏt'am* offerings of wedding feast food and cloth to the ancestors in her shrine. Without *yŏt'am,* the dead feel envy and frustration when the living indulge in celebratory feasting and lavish exchanges of goods. The unsettled dead are a common source of affliction and they may be inclined to follow the bride, bringing ominous influences to her new home.[2] Yongsu's Mother was particularly wary of her own dead husband and his first wife, the bride's parents. Because Yongsu's Mother is a shaman and holds numerous gods and ancestors in her shrine, she felt obliged to hold a particularly lavish and expensive *yŏt'am,* calling on one of her colleagues to assist her. She had given her dead husband lengths of silky synthetic fabric for spirit clothes instead of offering the customary scrap of a handkerchief that most of her clients provide. Yongsu's Mother grumbled about this, still with a touch of pride, as she itemized her laments over the cost and bother of marrying off a daughter. But even after making such a good show of the *yŏt'am,* something had gone terribly wrong.

Like the women who seek her services, she considered her present misfortune so unusual, so inexplicable as to suggest supernatural causation. Like her clients, she confirmed her hunch by tracing the onset of her misfortune to a ritual event, and like her clients, she sought out a *mansin* who could give her a divination. At a break in a *kut* that they were performing together, Yongsu's Mother asked the apprentice *mansin,* Okkyŏng's Mother, to divine the source of her misfortune. Okkyŏng's Mother had a vision of something aqua-blue that had been brought into the house. The vision was not surprising, the diagnosis common; meddlesome ghosts often ride into the house on cloth, clothing, or bright objects.[3] Yongsu's Mother thought that this must be the length of cloth she had given to her dead husband during the *yŏt'am.*

The dead husband remains an active presence in Yongsu's Mother's life and practice. His spirit resides on a little shelf just outside the shrine, and when Yongsu's Mother performs *kut,* he often appears in the guise of the Spirit Warrior, one of her gods. Once, in a dream, he had dictated the location of her shrine.[4] More recently, he had tugged on the rings in her newly pierced ears and caused an irritation because, Yongsu's Mother giggled, he had assumed that she was prettying up to remarry. Yongsu's Mother intended to use the length of *yŏt'am* cloth for a suit of Korean clothes or a formal overcoat but had been too busy to take the cloth to a tailor. Now she wondered if her husband's impatience was the source of her trouble. Perhaps she felt guilty, for she did still think of remarriage.

On the day after her divination, Okkyŏng's Mother called on Yongsu's Mother while I was visiting. Anxious to get to the bottom of things, Yongsu's Mother went out to her husband's shelf on the veranda and pulled down the cardboard box that held the new cloth offered in the *yŏt'am.* But when she unfurled the gauzy goods, Okkyŏng's Mother said, "That's not it, it's something in the inner room." Yongsu's Mother went back inside, unlocked her large wardrobe cabinet, and fished through the clothing piled within. She drew out a white Korean blouse and long aqua skirt and threw them to the floor with a vehement curse.

This must be it, the only aqua clothing in the chest, the Korean dress she had purchased for her eldest stepdaughter. Yongsu's Mother was angry. She spoke quickly. The whole family should wear new clothes in the wedding hall, but she had known that this was beyond her eldest stepdaughter's means. The woman had thanked her for the gift, but she had never come to take the dress away. Yongsu's Mother said, "I'll take it to the outhouse." Okkyŏng's Mother mentioned throwing salt and chanting. I was confused, and curious.

After Okkyŏng's Mother left, Yongsu's Mother continued to mutter, "It must be that. The dress and the cloth are the only new things that have come in. My husband couldn't be so angry with me. He wouldn't do that to me. Why should he keep his own wife from earning a living?" And then she announced in a loud voice, "I'm going out to take a piss." She carried the dress, still in the dressmaker's plastic bag, out with her, but returned with her arms full of laundry. She had left the bag behind.

I asked her what was going on, and she told me how Okkyŏng's Mother had seen a vision of aqua-blue clothing, how she had thought it was the cloth for her husband, and how she could not fathom her stepdaughter's having left the dress behind, "That fucking woman! Why is she such a slut? Last year I went to so many *kosa,*
and now . . ."

"What happened?"

"A restless spirit is active."

"Which one?"

"An *ancestral* restless spirit," (didn't the anthropologist understand that much?).

"Which ancestor?"

"That woman's mother, of course. It's because she died young."

Yongsu's Mother told me that she had "thrown the dress away in the outhouse," and giggled. This was a feint to put off the troublesome shade. Later, she asked me to bring the bag and its contents back inside. She had set them inside the shed but a safe distance from the foul pit. She washed her face and feet, performed an exorcism, and then we took the bag to the market and sought out the eldest stepdaughter. She was not at her usual place among the hawkers of rice cake, but Yongsu's Mother recognized a woman from the stepdaughter's village. She handed the bag over, asked the woman to deliver it, then walked away with a decisive step and an air of having settled something.

The stepdaughter's oversight was probably a rebuke; she would not accept her young stepmother's charity. The two women, never on good terms, had mustered a brave show of cordiality for the younger stepdaughter's wedding. There had been awkward moments. The stepdaughter, with the leathery complexion of a country market woman, looks older and far less attractive than her well-groomed stepmother, a woman embarrassingly close to her own age. At the engagement party they were presented to the groom's family, stood, and bowed in unison; a tactic aimed at rendering their respective statuses ambiguous and deflecting unflattering comparisons.

At the family party celebrating the bride's first visit home, Yongsu's Mother playfully teased the stepdaughter's children, but she made this slip, "You don't come to Auntie's house very often . . . er, I mean Grandmother's house . . ." She did not *feel* like their grandmother and there was no sustained relationship. Several months prior to these events, Yongsu's Mother had vented her many tribulations as a stepmother and her profound dislike of her eldest stepdaughter. A few years ago, when the stepson had finished grammar school, Yongsu's Mother bought him a cow to raise, but he soon abandoned the enterprise for factory employment, leaving her to sell the cow at a loss. Yongsu's Mother claims that the eldest stepdaughter encouraged the stepson to run away, "That woman isn't your mother. She's just your stepmother *(sŏmo)*, so why should you stay with her?"[5] Yongsu's Mother smarts at this remembered injustice, claims that she had nursed the little boy at her own breast, that he had always thought of her as his own mother, that he had never really known otherwise. "Why should that one come and tell him these things and make him run away?"

For more than a year she had refused to let the first son come home. "I was so mad, I told him, 'I took your shit and piss and raised you as though you were my own son, but you said that I was just a stepmother, and left.' He cried and cried and said that he wanted to see his mother so much he could die. Now he comes by and hangs around."

The stepdaughter has also asked her for forgiveness, perhaps anticipating her younger sister's inevitable marriage and the major role that Yongsu's Mother would be expected to play.

Yongsu's Mother claims that the woman approached her in the market saying, "Mother, forgive me, I'm so sorry, I didn't know what I was doing." But this did not keep Yongsu's Mother from having her say. "I went to your family and I raised you all. I didn't do you any wrong, but you ran away and caused your father to die of drink." ("How he drank!" she interpolates in the retelling, "He smashed all the plates in the cabinet and bashed in the door.") "What do you mean by coming over and telling your brother to run away? What right have you to return to your natal home?" The stepdaughter promised to visit during the New Year holiday and pay her respects, but Yongsu's Mother told her not to come. What if she started encouraging Yongsu, her own child, to run away? "It's no use raising other people's children," was Yongsu's Mother's summation. "If you do ten things right and make just one mistake, they say you've done badly by them because you're just a stepmother."

The eldest stepdaughter made trouble almost from the start of Yongsu's Mother's married life, and this story, told to the anthropologist to win sympathy, was told and retold to women who visited the house in the winter of Yongsu's Mother's bad luck.[6]

At first, Okhwa and I shared the housework. She cooked when I did the housework and when I cooked she did the housework. She was twenty-one years old then. I was married on the nineteenth day of the last (lunar) month, and on the fifteenth day of the New Year, they celebrated the end of the mourning period in the main house (the *k'ŭnjip,* the senior brother or uncle's household). I pressed my husband's formal jacket and he told the daughter, "Go on ahead and help them out."[7] When I got to the main house, Okhwa wasn't there. I said, "This is strange, she went out early." When my husband arrived, she was still missing. "Where did they say she's gone?" "She hasn't even been here."

He said, "I'll go back home and look for her. You stay here." I stayed and helped in the kitchen and he went back home but then neither he nor the daughter returned. He hadn't returned by evening when they set up for the *chesa* offering to the ancestors. Finally, my husband arrived. I asked, "Was Okhwa there?" She wasn't. The other children had seen her leave the house carrying a big, white bundle. The men were doing their *chesa* bows, but this gentleman, my husband, just stood at the side staring off into space. His soul had taken flight. Until that time, no maiden in the Yun family had ever run away. They were so concerned with proper behavior that in the past the women couldn't even go outside the big gate; no matter how hot it was, they could only mope around inside. It was a disgrace for the daughter of such a *yangban* house to run away.[8] From that moment my husband seemed to go crazy.

He told me to eat with the children at the big house and then come back home with the senior mother (his eldest brother's wife). My senior sister-in-law told him to have supper, but he took off without eating anything. By the time we had fed the kids and I arrived back home, he was up to his neck in liquor. [She raises her eyebrows.]

He was so drunk he didn't even recognize me. I went into the kitchen and started to light the fire, but he accosted me, "Who are you? What do you mean by coming into someone's kitchen and lighting the fire?" He was that far gone. I was dumbfounded. Good grief, his pockets were stuffed with *soju* bottles. I stood by, speechless, while he kicked in the door and broke the one forlorn little shrimp paste dish in the empty cabinet. He lambasted me and pissed, shhh, shhh, like that all night. He didn't know what he was doing, he couldn't tell one thing from another. And all night I went back and forth between crying and trying to reason with him and crying some more.

At dawn my senior sister-in-law came over with the nieces and nephews. Having been reviled all night, I was so relieved to see her that I ran outside in my bare feet and cried on her shoulder. Even if it was the death of me, I could not go on living in that house! I had never said a harsh word to Okhwa, what did she mean by running away? Since she'd taken off, it was unendurable to stay there. My husband had drunk all the bottles of *soju* that were in his pockets. When I counted them, there were sixteen bottles. He'd drunk them all down, so what could one expect? He was shivering and shaking, his chest was heaving, his face was drained and white, he kept saying, "I'm so cold, I'm so cold."

After they had finished the dawn *chesa*[9] in the main house, all of the cousins and everyone else came over. One of the senior brothers covered my husband with a quilt and sat on him and I knelt down beside him and tried to pin him down with my hands, but still he shivered so much that he was bouncing up and down. The cousin's wife in the next house brought over some sweet barley water and he gulped it down, not even realizing how hot it was; his lips puffed up with blisters. He lambasted me steadily until the next morning, and then he began to come back to his senses. He asked for a cigarette, but his hand shook when he held it. I asked him what he meant by all of this. We took him to the hospital and he had an injection. They told me to watch out for him because if he kept on behaving this way, it would be the end of him. I said, "Do you really think he'd stop drinking on my account?"

The very next morning, just as it was getting light, he went out again. He came back drunk and announced that he was going to throw himself into the river and drown. All the nephews and nephews' wives, all the grandchildren tried to hold him back so that he couldn't throw himself into the river. He was living on liquor. But then sometimes he was very subdued; he wouldn't say much at all. Sometimes he would just sit with a glazed look on his face. He was so ashamed because in all the Yun family there had never been a daughter who had run away like Okhwa. He was tense, always anticipating people's talk, the gossip that a daughter of the Yun family had run away.

When he wasn't drunk, he'd say that he had done me a great wrong in bringing me to his house and making me suffer these hardships. "What's the use?" he would say, "I brought you here to satisfy my own needs, and now my daughter's gone." But even as he said these things, he'd get all worked up about it and start drinking again, and soon enough the drinking broke his health.

After he'd gone on drinking like that for a few years, didn't that wretch of a daughter come back! Words can't express (her brazenness). I said, "When you see the state your father's in, you'll really regret what you've done." He was cutting weeds in the rice field when someone told him, "Your daughter's here." He ran to the house, waving his knife and shouting, "I'm going to kill her!" He was about to strike but I grabbed the knife and ran out of the room with it.

I sent Okhwa to her little mother's (the junior uncle's wife's) house. Normally, a man doesn't even talk to his younger brother's wife, but my husband ran right up to the house and screamed, "Send her out! Send her out!" The senior mother said, "This fucking woman, he'd just begun to settle down again, and now she's come back and caused all this commotion."

After three years of marriage, I was finally able to go and visit my own family. While I was back in Willow Market, I received a letter from the senior mother saying that Okhwa couldn't stand it at home any longer and had run away again. If we mentioned this to the father of my children, he'd fly off and say he was going to kill her. The senior mother had sent me Okhwa's address and I went right out to find her; I didn't even take the time to eat breakfast.

I saw Okhwa strolling along the path with a baby on her back. "What baby is this?" I asked. She was a maid-of-all-work and the baby belonged to her employers. I told her, "I'm not going to say anything more about it. Either you come with me or you don't and that's that. Your father is sick and there's nothing that can be done to change it."

Okhwa said, "I'll go with you even if it's the death of me. I'll go with you, Mother, and you can marry me off to anyone you choose, even to an A-frame carrier."[10] I took her to my mother's house in Willow Market and left her there. When I explained the actual circumstances of my marriage, my elder sister was shocked.

When I got back home, my children's father said, "Why are you so late?" I told him that I had run an errand in such and such a place. "I don't like to have a young wife like you gadding about."

"The senior mother asked me to do something for her; how could I refuse?"

"When you're not here, I don't even feel like going into the house."

I didn't say anything about Okhwa. I thought it over all night, and in the morning I went to the senior mother and told her that I had left Okhwa with my own family in Willow Market.

"What should I do?"

"If he knows, he'll raise another ruckus. Times are tough, otherwise I'd sell some rice to get cash for her."

And here the story breaks off. Having related all of Okhwa's infractions, Yongsu's Mother tells her audience in a low but emphatic voice, "That woman raised the wind, she fooled around." This is Yongsu's Mother's story; Okhwa would undoubtedly tell a different tale, perhaps of a wicked stepmother who drove her out of the house.

Okhwa did have a respectable wedding. The family photograph album holds a portrait of Okhwa masked in white bride's makeup with red dots on her cheeks and forehead. She looks glum, but this tells us nothing, for brides in those days were not supposed to smile. To highlight her difficulties in single-handedly planning the younger stepdaughter's wedding, Yongsu's Mother once conjured an image of herself and her husband cozily discussing Okhwa's wedding preparations across their common sleeping pallet. I noted at the time that this picture jarred with her usual portrayal of her short and fractious married life.

Throughout the winter of her bad fortune, Yongsu's Mother grumbled about her stepchildren. Clients came to see her, but now her health was bad. She had "used her nerves so much" over the younger stepdaughter's wedding, and then, in the thick of things, her stepson had an attack of acute appendicitis. She rushed off to Seoul and spent several days nursing him with yet more worry, more bother, more expense. And inevitably, when she launched into this topic, some long or short fragment of the story of her eldest stepdaughter would tumble out. The younger stepchildren had worn her down; she had "used her nerves," worried, fretted, brooded, and this was the cause of the diarrhea and indigestion that plagued her all January.[11] More generally, stepchildren are nothing but trouble, so on to the story of the one who ran away and drove her own father to drink. But how was the eldest stepdaughter responsible for Yongsu's Mother's professional dry season? How was the intrusion of the first wife's shade the stepdaughter's fault? The connection appears in another of Yongsu's Mother's stories, one she told me in bits and pieces to illustrate the power of restless ancestors, at length to pass the time that winter, and yet again in the summer of 1983 on the night of the first wife's *chesa*.

I saw her when my husband was sick, no, even before he was sick. It was when I first married into that house. Every night a woman with a child on her back would come and sit on the porch just outside the inner room. Since I was newly married, what did I know about these things? She was always there, sitting on the porch. I thought, "This isn't a good dream." You see, it was my husband's first wife who was sitting there on the porch.

Then my husband was sick and my stepson was sick. The boy was her son, wasn't he? If the father wasn't sick, the son was sick, and if the son wasn't sick, the father was sick. We did exorcisms *(p'udakkŏri)* and more exorcisms and then *kut.* When the stepson was five years old he caught the measles. The red blemishes came out and blossomed, but they didn't go away. They're supposed to go away. The boy's fever was over 104 degrees. Such a frightening fever! He was a ball of fire.

We took him to the hospital and they gave him an injection. It seemed as though the fever was going down bit by bit. But then the next day, the senior mother and father had a look at him and said he was dying. They told me to place him on the cold side of the floor and cover him with a quilt. His shit came out black. I showed it to the senior mother, the third elder brother's wife. She said, "They say that when a child's shit is black like that, he's going to die. He's a child that's not meant to live; you should just lay him out."

I went to the boy's father and I said, "We've gone to the hospital and that didn't work. I want to go somewhere and see if I can get a divination." The boy's father jumped up, "He's all but dead already, and you say you're going for a divination. We don't do that sort of thing here." I told him not to be so stubborn, but he wouldn't let me go.

The senior mother went to him and said, "Brother-in-law, don't be this way when your child's on the brink of death. Won't you do anything possible to save him? Let her go and try."

I went, and the shaman said we should clean up the measles' influences *(hongyŏk subi)*. I went back and told my husband, but he just said, "What beggar's talk is this?" I was young. What did I know? I went to the senior mother.

"What shall we do?"

"What did the shaman say?"

"She says that if we do an exorcism, the boy will live. It's because of his mother's death. There are (inauspicious) things that must be cast away."

My husband said, "This is stupid talk, the boy's all but dead. What's the point of saying that you want to hold an exorcism?" But the senior mother-in-law coaxed him and I coaxed him, and then we set up two offering trays and I set out the exorcism rice, some vegetables, and the wine. The shaman sat there with a winnowing basket, the kind they used to use. She sat on the veranda chanting a little bit of something, and scratching the basket. The senior mother and I sat there listening to her, but the boy's father went off somewhere. It was all over by ten-thirty in the evening. I saw the shaman home and the senior mother watched the house. When I returned, my husband returned.

"What foolishness was that? What was the point of it?"

"Husband, we've spent the money, and now it's done. We did it so that even if the boy dies, there won't be any resentment. (His soul won't carry a grudge, since we've done everything we can for him.)"

We'd brought it off, and that night the child slept. But how could I sleep? I was so anxious. At dawn the child mumbled something, "Mother, let me have some water." I brought in some boiled water and gave him a spoonful. He'd swallowed a spoonful of water. He hadn't died.

I knew that I wouldn't be able to sleep, so I told my husband, "You watch the child; I'm going to fix the rice." He was still sleepy. [She yawns in the telling.] He was surprised that I would think of fixing breakfast so early in the morning. I was cooking the rice when he called me back in. "The boy's asking for something." He wanted more water. By that time, the rice was boiling away. I took some of the rice water, put in some sugar, and took it to him saying, "Here, try this." He drank about half a cup and I said, "Well, this kid's going to live." I felt ill at ease, though. I was glad that the child would live, but it was strange.

I gave him more rice water, and bit by bit, the rash went away just beautifully. My husband said, "Isn't it odd, they said he was going to die, and now the fever's gone and he's eating."

"He may die yet."

"Oh no, not if he's eating like this. He isn't going to die."

We were careful. We gave him only small amounts of rice because he hadn't eaten for a long time. But whenever he ate anything, he would cough and cough. He was weak; there was nothing we could do about it, so every morning I would take him to the hospital on my back while his father cooked the rice. The doctor was about ten li away and there wasn't any bus. I simply had to walk there with the boy on my back. When we returned, I didn't have the least bit of strength left, and I was hungry. My husband would have made the rice or, when he didn't feel like fixing rice, he'd just boil noodles.

For two weeks I took the boy to the hospital every morning to get an injection, and we brought home some medicine. After two weeks they told me at the hospital that if I took good care of the boy and fed him well, I wouldn't have to bring him back. We bought some beef. It wasn't so expensive then, but neither did we have very much money. We'd buy just a tiny lump of beef, boil it to make broth, and then make rice porridge in the broth. To nourish the child, I'd put in an egg and some sesame oil. Within three months, that boy was up and around. Within three months, with one hand in his father's hand and one hand in mine, he took one little step after another.

The boy lived and got better, but then his father got sick. He had nightmares. He was exhausted. He took Chinese medicine, but his digestion was always off so he took medicine for that. One night we were sleeping all together, the baby on the warm spot, then me, then my husband. All of a sudden and still in his sleep, my husband raised his fist and struck the floor. I was startled. I woke up and asked him what he meant by pounding the floor with his fist. He said, "Don't think badly of me."

"Badly of you?"

"Okhwa's mother, my dead wife, came into the room."

I was here, and my husband was there, and she came right in between us. He had yelled "Vile woman!" and tried to strike her. He had flailed at her and flailed at her, but his fist just struck the floor. [In 1985 she added this detail: the dead wife had puckered her lips for a kiss.][12]

I said, "This is strange. This is no ordinary dream. I often dream of a woman with a child on her back who sits on the porch. I feel uneasy when I have these dreams."

He said, "Can a dead person come back to life? Don't fret over it," but his condition went from bad to worse. He went to the hospital. Our senior cousin's wife went to a *posal* (inspirational diviner), who said to do an exorcism. I asked his permission, and went to the *posal*'s house, but even though we held an exorcism, my husband's health did not improve. [She omits the story of how her hands stuck fast to her sides.]

He got worse and worse. We would try this hospital and then try that hospital. At one place they would say his digestion was bad. At another place, they would say it was his liver. At still another, it was his bowels. They'd say this here and they'd say that there. You think that wasn't frustrating? And he just got worse and worse. My husband's stomach was bloated way out to here. We went to a Chinese doctor for a pulse reading, and they said he had to take his medicine diligently. Just one tablet was expensive, but still he took it, and that seemed to make him even worse. The senior mother told me not to give him any more of that medicine.

Then we went to Seoul, to some big hospital way out to the east of the city. What was the name of that place? At that hospital they said his problem was parasites! I thought, "If he takes the least bit of food, he runs to the outhouse. Parasites aren't like that. I don't think that's what it is." Next I took him to my old home in Willow Market. There was a hospital for Chinese medicine (Hanyak) nearby, where, every day, they read his pulse and gave him herbal tonics. The doctor in charge said, "This is difficult, very difficult to cure." So then didn't my children's father ask for a *kut!*

We held the *kut* in my mother's house. My mother sold a pig that she had been raising. On the day of the *kut,* my husband sat up and said, "I think I'm going to live." We did the *kut* and I thought to myself that he seemed better, but the next day he was even worse. The senior father and mother and the nieces and nephews came and took him to the university hospital in Seoul. At the hospital, they said that it was all because he had drunk so much, and they said that he would have to stay in the hospital.

He was so sick. What could I do? My two-year-old Yongsu was still nursing at my breast, so I took him on my back and went to tend my husband in the hospital. There I was, nursing my baby, and I fell asleep. Didn't that woman come back again! That ghost *(kwisin)* came right on into the hospital with her baby on her back.

It was the sixth day of the fifth month, her *chesa* day. Of course since we were at the hospital we hadn't held a *chesa* for her. She said, "I've come to eat."

"What do you mean, 'Come to eat'? We haven't fixed any rice."

"I'm going to stay right here. I'm going to the kitchen to get the rice measure." She went to the kitchen and came back in again.

In my dream, I had some of the sweet cake we call Costella bread. I had some of that sweet cake in my hand and was about to eat it when I thought to myself, "Why should I eat this? I should give it to the patient." I went over to my husband and said, "Dear, here's some cake. You'll take some, won't you? It's that Costella bread that you like so much. Try a little, won't you?"

"Cake?"

"Yes, have some. You have to eat and gather your strength."

He reached up for it, but that woman snatched it away. She said, "No! I'm going to take it away and eat it," and grabbed the cake just as my husband reached for it. [In another version of the story, when the dead first wife returns from the kitchen with the rice scoop, the ailing husband wakes suddenly, screams, and turns his face to the wall.]

I was startled awake. I was muttering to myself, "Such a strange, strange dream. Why should that woman come all the way to the hospital like that?" My husband asked what I meant by sitting there talking to myself, and I said, "Dear, it was so strange. I was sitting here holding some cake and that woman with the little girl on her back came in and asked for rice. She went to the kitchen and came back again. I wanted you to have some cake, but that woman came back and took it. Odd, did she come all this way just to eat?"

He brushed it off, but even in the hospital his health got worse. He went back to the hospital on the sixth day of the second (lunar) month but by the fourteenth day of the fourth month, they said that they could not cure him, and he came back home. After five nights at home, he died at four in the morning. After he died, I never again saw that woman in a dream. She had come to take her husband away with her. That woman took him away.

To corroborate this accusation, she told me the story of her sister-in-law's dream on Yongsu's Mother's wedding night. Again, I had heard another version of the story with a different emphasis (see chapter 6).

How did she die? I don't know. It was something to do with her insides. She gave birth to the boy who's nineteen years old now, and she died. The child on her back? She had a baby who died, so of course they go around together. [She answers my questions and plunges back into her story.]

They kept me up past midnight on my wedding night bowing to all the relatives. I was so exhausted I could have died. One of my sisters-in-law kept dozing off because it was so late. My sister-in-law dreamed that it was summer. Why should it be summer? I had married in the last month of the year. (In her dream) the whole front courtyard was in flames, so high that no one could get through. But there, in the midst of the fire, was someone clearing a path through the flames with the big halbard we use in *kut*. The dead woman was clearing a path from the front gate; the flames rose up on both sides of her. My sister-in-law called out to her, "You should cut down all the flames. Why are you just making a path?"

I was sitting in the inner room with all the grandfathers' (gods' and ancestors') costumes on a line above my head, the way we hang them at a *kut*. Rice and vegetables (offerings) had been set out, and I was sitting there hitting the hour-glass drum. (The dead woman said,) "What does your new sister-in-law think she's doing, this bride who has just come to her husband's house? Day and night, she just eats and hits the hour-glass drum. The cucumbers have all ripened in the field. Even though they're spoiling, she neither pickles them nor sets them to soak in brine. She just hits the drum."

My sister-in-law said, "Elder sister-in-law, please take care of things."

"Me? Why should I do that for her? Younger sister-in-law, you gather up the cucumbers and set them to soak."

"How can I do that? What if the new elder sister-in-law who arrived yesterday makes a fuss?"

"No, she won't."

My younger brother-in-law shook his wife awake, "Dear, dear, what were you dreaming?" and my sister-in-law saw that it was a dream. That woman came to take her husband away with her. She had even cleared a path. I married very badly.

Her closing comment ties together the stories she told in her winter doldrums. She married badly because she married into a house with an ominous restless ancestor, a dead first wife who returned to claim her husband, and she married badly because she was married to an impoverished drunkard, burdened with ungrateful stepchildren, and soon widowed. Although Yongsu's Mother has never (in my hearing) attributed Okhwa's early "raising the wind" to her dead mother's influence, she frequently blames a dead first wife for the unruliness of a client's stepchild, and the jealousy of a dead first wife for a husband's illness or death.[13] Okhwa ran away and her father drank himself to death in shame. The dead wife returned, cleared a path, and carried her husband away. The stories are not contradictory; their common end result, Yongsu's Mother's early widowhood, is the most dire consequence of her having "married badly."

The consequences of her bad marriage, a fusion of social and spiritual circumstances, define Yongsu's Mother's present. The eldest stepdaughter refused to accept her gift of a holiday dress, a slight rather than sorcery, but the stepdaughter's ill-humored act drew in the dead first wife's restless spirit and precipitated Yongsu's Mother's season of ill luck. Once defined, Yongsu's Mother could deal with her old adversary, cast out the ghost with a pelting of coarse grain and the slashing of a kitchen knife. But while she can hold the first wife's ghost at bay, she is stuck with this old ghost, just as she is stuck with her ungrateful stepchildren. Between the stepdaughter's wedding and the stepson's appendectomy, her stepchildren had worn her down, both financially and emotionally. They were also responsible, indirectly, for the depletion of her spiritual resources.

She had held an elaborate *yŏt'am* before the stepdaughter's wedding to settle the potentially disruptive spirits of her husband and his first wife. This strategy had backfired miserably. The eldest stepdaughter's thoughtlessness, leaving her new dress with Yongsu's Mother, had stirred up the dead first wife despite the offering feast of wedding noodles. And more was amiss in the shrine. Yongsu's Mother now believed that her gods and ancestors were impatient with her; she had held an elaborate *yŏt'am* and hit the hour-glass drum, roused them up without giving them the feasting and amusement of a *kut.* Although she had wanted to avoid the expense, she realized that this spring she would have to hold a flower-greeting *kut* for the pleasure of her own spirits.

Between stomach discomfort and worry, she was sleeping badly, and now she began to have unsettling dreams. "Last night I dreamed that I was holding three little jackets with rainbow sleeves (the clothes that children wear for their first birthday celebrations and shamans use to indicate the presence of smallpox spirits). I was climbing a mountain; there was a water wheel at the top spilling water over the summit. I could see a little boy and a little girl down below. Some grandfather shouted that everything would be all right if I threw the clothes over the ridge but I woke up still clutching them in my hands." It was obvious to Yongsu's Mother that the children were Child Messengers (Tongja Pyŏlsang), spirits of children who died of smallpox or measles and follow the Special Messenger; she told me again about the little sister who had died of smallpox. But why had she dreamed such a strange and seemingly portentous dream? She sent for the Clear Spring Mansin. The Clear Spring Mansin interpreted this dream as a sign of Yongsu's Father's displeasure. Yongsu's Mother had gone to a *kut* with a jacket that she had dedicated to the Spirit Warrior at her stepdaughter's *yŏt'am*. Had she worn this costume, Yongsu's Father would have appeared in the guise of the Spirit Warrior and played at the *kut,* but Yongsu's Mother had selected another costume when she performed this sequence. The Clear Spring Mansin went further, encouraging Yongsu's Mother to break with Chatterbox Mansin; Yongsu's Father disliked working in concert with the Chatterbox Mansin's guardian spirit. For her part, Yongsu's Mother had been complaining that Chatterbox exploited her, never paying her adequately although she performed the most demanding segments at Chatterbox's *kut.*

Yongsu's Father's displeasure was further confirmed when Yongsu's Mother dreamed of her neighbor, the widower Yun, who told her that she had suffered by herself long enough and that he was going to marry her. "Well of course," clucked the women to whom she related this dream, "He's another man named Yun, (just like your husband)"; the dream widower Yun was a stand-in for Yongsu's Father's discontented spirit. Influenced by different theories of dream interpretation, I was skeptical. I knew from village gossip that she had been courted by the widower Yun but that his hot-tempered daughter-in-law had spoiled the match.[14] For several months he had been avoiding Yongsu's Mother, who now used me to garner intelligence on the Yun household. A few weeks later she reported, "I dreamed that the widower Yun got married, and to a woman who was just a kid, only twenty-six or twenty-seven years old," her own age when she had married an older man named Yun. "All of the neighbors were bustling around, fixing the feast food. I thought, 'Why is she so young, young enough to be his youngest daughter? They'll have to live apart from that daughter-in-law. This bride must have a terrible fate to be the mother-in-law of such a daughter-in-law,' and when I woke up I was sobbing and sobbing, I don't know why." "Aha," I thought. But she gave this dream an impersonal interpretation. She had dreamed it in the shaman's capacity for dreaming portentous dreams about her clients. "This is a death dream; it doesn't mean anything good for that house. Have you been there recently? Is the widower Yun ill?"

A few nights after her dream of the rainbow-sleeved jackets, Yongsu's Mother dreamed a confirmation of the Clear Spring Mansin's advice that she break with Chatterbox Mansin. In her dream she saw Chatterbox and an unknown woman who gripped two cooked chickens in her teeth, gobbling them up; this was the incompatible guardian spirit. Yongsu's Mother was sleeping fitfully, troubled by stomach pain, and that same night she had also dreamed of her own father, dressed in white. A woman stood at his side, but in the dream Yongsu's Mother could not see if it was her mother or one of her sisters. She roused herself, boiled some millet, and set it beside her pillow as the first step in an exorcism. I asked her if she was going to send for the Clear Spring Mansin again, but she said no, the meaning of her dream was obvious, a sign of restless ancestors and a further indication of her weakened spiritual resources. "Why should I have such a dream? Whenever I dream of my natal family, no good comes of it. My father was no good when he was alive and it does me no good to see him now that he's dead."

The restless dead from old stories are a part of Yongsu's Mother's present; the disappointing husband, the meddlesome first wife, the irredeemable father all cast their shadows on her dreaming, waking life. But her stories also contain symbols of personal power drawn from a rich cultural lexicon. Just as she would advise her clients, having probed their dreams and her own visions, she began to devise a strategy to purify herself of overwhelmingly negative influences and revitalize her working relationship with the gods in her shrine. In the fall, when things began to go wrong, she had planned to pray at the Immortal's Rock in her old neighborhood, the sacred spot that she had visited compulsively during her late adolescent illness. When neighbors polluted the cluster of households by killing a dog to make tonic soup, the trip had been postponed. Now, on the day after the two inauspicious dreams, Yongsu's Mother announced that she was planning to use the mountain, to make offerings at the shrine on the hillside behind the village. She told me that she had thought it over, how she would begin to get better and then, oddly, relapse, how her moods were bad, how nothing had worked out since the stepdaughter's wedding. We would go up to the village shrine in the New Year and begin things fresh and clean. As a confirmation of her intentions, she dreamed of climbing the hillside and setting out her offerings in the snow.

Around this time I also had a vivid dream, late one snowy afternoon. In my dream, it was also dusk and snowing lightly. I saw a white canvas tent, the kind griddle cake vendors set up on Korean streets, but this tent was on the edge of a forest. Light from inside the tent glowed through the canvas and snowflakes sparkled in the aura. When I walked inside, the shimmer of numerous candles suffused the tent with golden light. Yongsu's Mother and several village women were there, older women with browned faces and hair bound up under towels. I recognized Grandmother Song from the next hamlet, who often stopped by the *mansin*'s house to chat. The women were all eating griddle cake and wanted me to stay and have some. In the dream, I felt that I ought not to stop, that I ought to continue interviewing, but it was pleasant and warm inside the tent, while outside it was snowing. They offered me a warm cake. I thought, "If I eat this sort of thing, I'll get fat." When I woke up, I hadn't tasted the cake, but neither had I gone back out into the snow. I woke up hungry for griddle cake.

I told this dream to Yongsu's Mother on the night we visited the village shrine. "You have dreamed well." Snow falling in the dream was white like rice; I would not have to worry about food. The candle light inside the tent blazed from the four directions, auspicious for the accomplishment of all my desires. The shaman was especially pleased that I saw her with a knot of village grandmothers. These must be her own "grandmothers," the female deities from her shrine, who were now especially pleased with me because I had worshipped them. Grandmother Song probably represented the Village Shrine Grandmother (Todang Halmŏni). Do we not offer rice cake in the snow at her shrine and light candles there?[15]

And so it was that on the cold January midnight of a lunar New Year we left the village and found the path that we had brushed in the snow that afternoon. Yongsu was with us, carrying the cooking equipment, but the stepson, home for the holiday, was left behind to watch the house. We climbed up to the shrine in the dark and lighted a bonfire; I worried that the light would provoke anticommunist patrols but Yongsu's Mother reassured me, "They know that there's been a village shrine here from long ago." We cooked our rice, drew water from the well, and arranged simple offerings, vegetables, candies, and a few pieces of fruit. Yongsu's Mother set Yongsu and me to bowing while she invoked the gods of the shrine, who promised us splendid futures. She tossed sugar-candy chestnuts to divine her own fortune and, as her proxy, I caught them in my lap. It was bitterly cold when the last wailing ghost had been sent off from the shrine tree. With a lighter step, Yongsu's Mother led the way down the hill, casting off scraps of offering food while she chanted the wandering dead and other noxious influences from our path.

EPILOGUE

1985

Yongsu's Father, bearing the titles of Body-Governing Spirit Warrior and Great Spirit Warrior (Sinjang Momju, Taesin Sinjang), in his official capacity as the guardian god of Yongsu's Mother's shrine, speaks through the lips of a *mansin* and laments his early death, "A *yangban* such as I, and in my youth . . ."[1]

"Typhoid take that!" snaps Yongsu's Mother from behind the drum. "You're always going on about your noble origins, '*yangban, yangban.*' "

"But I am of *yangban* stock."

"And a *mudang*'s been possessed right in a nook of your *yangban* house."

She snaps back her complaints. He thinks he has problems. She has to earn a living and if he won't help her, she'll just see about getting herself a better husband. Yongsu's Father rubs his belly, "If it weren't for this, I'd be alive today."

"Well, you drank." She gives him no quarter as the baleful laments continue, interspersed with the prognostications that Yongsu's Father bestows, in his role as the guardian god, on the *mansin* and assembled guests. With characteristic sweetness, Okkyŏng's Mother offers him some Bacchus, a caffeine tonic that the *mansin* consume in great quantities during *kut*.

"You think he knows what Bacchus is? Was there Bacchus back then? He didn't know about Bacchus. He drank nothing but rotgut vodka."

"You've affronted my *yangban* honor. You haven't even given me any snacks with my wine. Hey, let's take our socks off."

"What's the point if we take them off?"

"Like the good old days."

"You bet, like the good old days. What's the point?"

He is still with her, and the relationship remains contentious, a story played and replayed in the bantering drama of her *kut.* As the guardian god of her shrine, Yongsu's Father is a public spirit whose presence carries far greater consequence than that of an ordinary and personal ancestor. Yongsu's Mother's colleagues, her clients, and the anthropologist have all encountered Yongsu's Father, though none of us knew the man when he was alive. When he appears as her Body-Governing Spirit Warrior, the Great Spirit Warrior of her shrine, he tells us things of consequence, and once during my early fieldwork, he made trouble for me because I had neglected to fill his wine cup while making offerings to her other gods. Thereafter, over the years, whenever I return to Yongsu's Mother's house, I make a great show of pouring out his wine and greeting him with a full kowtow. On my most recent trip, when I made offerings in the shrine, he was invoked, spoke through Yongsu's Mother, and wept over me. "Why did Yongsu's Father cry?" I asked when the ritual was over and Yongsu's Mother herself again. She said he was touched that I had come to the shrine. "Both you and I are lonely. You don't have siblings, and while I have siblings, I'm living as a widow. You come to Korea from a great distance and seek out the shrine grandfathers. He thinks this is sweet. He's grateful." I jot in my notebook, "we are deep in our own metaphor," as when, with divine voice, she chides me for darting off here and there on new research and not having time for the spirits (or Yongsu's Mother).

But there are other clients and other metaphors. The day after our tearful encounter in the shrine, Yongsu's Father appeared at a *kut* and harangued a young man with a drinking problem, "Don't do as I did." Instead of pouring out the customary cup of wine, he handed the sheepish client an apple from the offering tray—"This will refresh your insides"—amid a soft chorus of chuckles.

Despite her threats to get herself a better husband if her guardian god and spouse does not bring her more business, Yongsu's Mother seems reconciled to her situation. Now she rationalizes. A junior colleague, a rare maiden *mansin,* was much aggrieved over the difficulty of finding a husband, while the Songjuk Mansin incurred divine displeasure when her prodigal husband returned after an absence of twenty years. The ailing and ever-jealous husband of Okkyŏng's Mother was "just a worry pit." "When you think about it," mused Yongsu's Mother, "it's difficult for a *mansin* to marry. Look at me, I've been single since I was twenty-nine. I'd like to have a husband. Isn't that what people do? But most of the gods are men, and they get their dander up. Besides, people say that a *mansin*'s husband is a good-for-nothing who fools around with his wife's money." She thrust her hands behind her back and spun around in imitation of the greedy and vexatious Official (Taegam) she portrays in *kut,* a gesture that seemed to characterize the capricious tempers of both god and man.

But Yongsu's Mother is doing quite well on her own. In 1981 she left her dark little metal-roofed house. The government had widened the road through the village, compensating those, like Yongsu's Mother, who had lost their land and encouraging them to build modern bungalows. Yongsu's Mother chose to make a statement; combining her savings with the compensation money, she built herself a splendid house set back behind a high iron gate with a doorbell that pealed music. There were decorative plants in her front garden and in pots on the stairway leading up to her door. A bright, spacious, wooden-floor room opened on to three hot-floor rooms, a commodious kitchen, and a tiled bath. Lace curtains hung in the windows, framing a fanciful sculpture of macrame and artificial flowers, a gift from the Willow Market Daughter. There was running water in the kitchen and bath, and when I last visited Yongsu's Mother, she was installing a hot water boiler, "so that we can bathe every day the way you do in America."

The house was a turning point for Yongsu's Mother and she noted, to draw a parallel, that she had changed her residence in the same year that I had married. The house now marked her as a wealthy person, a person of consequence, and a target of envy. "Come and visit," her neighbors would tell me, "but, of course, our house isn't anything like Yongsu's Mother's." She was cynical about the attention she now received from her husband's kin, the flood of invitations to weddings and birthdays, and the fuss that uncles, aunts, and cousins made over Yongsu whenever he returned to visit his father's grave. "When I was raising those kids, did anyone so much as buy us a pair of socks?"

In 1985 she installed a direct-dial telephone for the convenience of her many clients and bought a color television set. As a consequence of these purchases, she could not afford to host a flower-greeting *kut* this year; a pilgrimage to the mountain would suffice. Recalling her troubles in 1977, I marveled at her new self-confidence. But the grandfathers and grandmothers of the shrine had also benefited by her success. This same year she had replaced the little white plaster Buddhas with larger, more imposing gold-painted images, which she escorted from Seoul in three taxis and installed in the shrine with due ceremony. For the installation, she had covered their heads with white cowls and draped their bodies with blue and red thread. The cowls could be worn as grave clothes and she kept one for this purpose, making gifts of the rest to Chatterbox, their mother, and her new colleague, the Songjuk Mansin. She distributed pieces of red and blue thread among the fifty-seven clients who had contributed funds for the installation of the Buddhas and placed some in Yongsu's pocket when he sat for the university entrance examination. Even so, she noted with chagrin, Yongsu had failed, although he scored well and might have been successful had he aspired to a less prestigious school. "He doesn't have school luck or job luck," she muttered, "just girl luck."

Yongsu's Mother now claims more than eighty regular clients *(tan'gol)*, although some of these were inherited from her sister, who gave up her practice in a disappointing attempt to live with one, then another married son. Chatterbox Mansin's grandmothers and grandfathers were installed in Yongsu's Mother's shrine, but like the two *mansin* sisters of forceful personality, the two sets of gods could not reside in close quarters without conflict. After the installation of Chatterbox's pantheon, Yongsu's Mother had disturbing dreams. Three women came to her for a divination session and she brought out the divining tray, covered with rice and coins. One woman sat to have her fortune told but the other two insisted on standing, watching her from the side. Yongsu's Mother felt uncomfortable as she began to toss the coins and rice and seek her visions in the resulting configurations. Then one of the women grabbed the rice, the Great Spirit Grandmother's rice, and scattered it on the floor of the shrine. Yongsu's Mother felt deeply offended for the god's sake.

Chatterbox interpreted her dream as the sign of a quarrel among the two pantheons; the woman who had spilled the rice was probably the Jade Immortal, her own abandoned god whose picture had been unceremoniously installed under that of Yongsu's Mother's Great Spirit Grandmother. Yongsu's Mother separated the pictures and gave the Jade Immortal her own place in the shrine. This was not the end of divine quarrels. Chatterbox's Body-Governing God, a distant grandmother from her natal home, had been placed with Yongsu's Father on his separate shelf above the new refrigerator. The new god was intended as a Great Spirit Wife (Taesin Manura), Chatterbox told me with a giggle, but of course the two gods quarreled, as they had in the past, and their sets of spirit clothes were now stored separately. In the summer of 1983, during the offerings made to the Seven Stars, the Great Spirit Wife possessed Yongsu's Mother and stomped over to Yongsu's Father's shelf, where she scowled and clashed her cymbals. "Our grandmother makes a lot of noise," Chatterbox remarked, amused.

That same summer, Yongsu's Mother was again suffering from precarious health and a slow professional season, although things were not nearly so serious as they had been at the end of 1977. A *mansin* who visited the new house told her that her luck would change if she moved her shrine from the side room to the center room. An auspicious day was chosen, Yongsu's desk and cabinet were removed, my husband and I carried the books and bags of our summer residence from center to side, carpenters were called in, and a new shrine established in the center room. That night Yongsu's Mother served up an offering of red bean porridge to mark a change in residence.

On the eve of the seventh day of the seventh lunar month, Yongsu's Mother made her own offerings in the shrine and summoned up the gods, who told her why they had been dissatisfied with the side room. They were aristocratic gods, they said, real *yangban,* but she had housed them in side quarters as if they had been servants or hired laborers. With their elevated sense of propriety, they were further vexed that she appeared before them in her bare feet and wearing a short Western skirt. *Mansin* with more common gods could do as they pleased, but she should greet hers in proper Korean dress and wearing fresh white padded socks. The next day, in the August heat, she wore the appropriate socks but had not capitulated to the point of wearing a hot and cumbersome Korean dress. She delighted in telling her clients about the gods' complaints, transforming her old impatience with her husband's undue concern for propriety into a matter of pride. Cynical neighbors commented that she had merely wanted to free up the side room, which had adjoining kitchen space and could be rented out. "We'll just see what she does with that room," an envious neighbor muttered, but mother and son preferred not to take in strangers. She was reluctantly contemplating renting the room two years later, when Yongsu left home to join the army.

With her own success and Chatterbox's disappointing retirement, Yongsu's Mother was again the mainstay of her natal family. Her younger brother, by law and custom the head of the family, had immigrated to the United States, leaving his children with their grandmother in Willow Market and writing all too infrequently. Yongsu's Mother, responsible for her own mother and her brother's children, told me that she wanted to go to America and pop him one right in the face. And she worried now about her elder sister, the overbearing patron of her younger years, who had surrendered her powers but found no comfortable home with her ungracious daughters-in-law. The roles were reversed; it was now Yongsu's Mother who, from a position of strength, contemplated her sister's uncertain future. "I tell her I'm going to marry her off," she jokes. "Why not?" I reply. "After all, didn't she marry you off?" Yongsu's Mother laughs, but my remark does not trigger the old angry story of her marriage. I have not heard that story now for several years. Instead, she remembers past kindnesses, how her sister fed her meat to build up her strength when she came back to visit her natal home.

Her sister's fate, and examples of other women who have suffered at the mercy of strong-willed daughters-in-law, make Yongsu's Mother apprehensive of her own future. In the fall of 1985 Yongsu was at home, loafing about at loose ends while he waited to join the army. Since the spring Yongsu had been dating a bubbly young woman whom he had met at a cram school. "Dating, dating," Yongsu's Mother would rage when Yongsu touched her up for cash, "did we date in the old days?" "In the old days," said Yongsu, "I'd already be married and have a son." Appreciating the logic and wit of this, Yongsu's Mother entered his remark into her repertoire.

But alas, the girlfriend comes from a Christian house, and Yongsu's Mother is horrified at the prospect of a daughter-in-law who will not pray on the mountain. "In this house, with our gods and ancestors, we have to do those things." It was a pity, she conceded, since the young man and woman were so clearly attracted to each other. Concerned for Yongsu's happiness, she could not muster much optimism for her own golden years. Why should she? She has endured hardship from the time she was a baby and her mother, exhausted from carrying her around on her back while she worked, never had enough milk for her. Thus, from the start, she has been weak and sickly and does not anticipate a long life. "When I die, I want to be reborn in a rich family. I wasn't able to study. I never had the love of parents, of siblings, of a husband, none of it, none of it." (Was she saying, "Next time around I want your life"?)

"You enjoy the love of your child," I suggested hopefully. "Well, yes, Yongsu helps me now but we'll just see how things turn out when he's married. We have to bring in a good daughter-in-law. These days they just abuse you. I haven't been lucky in any other relationship, so why should I be blessed with my daughter-in-law? I don't want to stick around to be abused, thinking sad thoughts about my past and brooding over the present. I'll marry off my son and see my grandchildren, and then, *pok,* I'll die." She rolls up her eyes, jerks her head to the side, and makes a comic gesture of her own demise.

I went back to Yongsu's Mother's house in 1985 to tell her that I had finally translated the story of her life, to see if she was still willing to have me publish it, and to ask her help in completing the manuscript. I brought her a copy of my first book, inscribed "to my *mansin* honorable teacher," and heard her cap a discussion with "I've even come out in a book in America." We went to the mountain and to *kut.* I did the sort of things I had done while working on my dissertation and enjoyed the comfortable sensation of treading familiar terrain. But days passed before I could explain to Yongsu's Mother the real purpose of my visit. I wanted to be certain that she understood what I was about, and I wanted to discuss this project in privacy. This last condition was difficult to achieve in her sociable inner room, but one afternoon, when the last guest had departed and just before Yongsu returned home from another date, I brought out one of the old tapes and slipped it into my machine.

"You still have those old things?" "Listen, do you hear the trucks going by your old house?" She listens, amused, but without the interest provoked by recordings of her recent *kut.* I tell her about the translations and about the book I plan to publish. "But in America, what if Koreans read it? They'll think it's shameful." Her world has broadened. When I first knew her, America was on the other side of the earth, the home of the odd-complected soldiers who ran in formation on the road by her house, a land she had seen in movies. In 1985, America is where her brother and the kin of her neighbors live, a place where Koreans live. Appreciating her concern, I take a deep breath. I want to protect her and perhaps it is safest to abandon the project, but I also want her to know the worth of her storytelling. "Americans won't find it shameful; they'll think it's interesting, as interesting as a novel." "As interesting as a novel," she repeats the phrase to herself. "It has social and historical significance," I continue, using a Korean vocabulary that I read rather than speak, the words that do not ordinarily enter village conversation. "Of course, there are people who are incapable of understanding. I know this. I don't want any harm to come to you or Yongsu. As I have done in the past, I will try to keep your name a secret. In the book I've called you 'Yongsu's Mother.' When my friends from Seoul came here for the *kut* the other day, they kept asking, 'Where's Yongsu's Mother?' " She laughs, and agrees to help me.

I was leaving again. In the company of Songjuk Mansin, about to depart for a *kut,* Yongsu's Mother presented me with some Korean accoutrements for my American kitchen. She gave me a pair of covered rice bowls—a high *chubal,* such as men use, and a woman's short broad *hap*—and a large, then a smaller rice pot, "so that your husband can cook rice when you are away." She saw the very un-Korean premise of my married life and was amused.

"What's her husband like?"

"Nice, steady going," said Yongsu's Mother, and told a story from our visit in the summer of 1983. "It was the middle of the day, no one was around. I heard a faint splashing sound in the bath . . . I tiptoed in . . . And there was the husband doing the laundry!"

The prospect of my husband quietly doing laundry to surprise his absent wife was an image so droll as to provoke extended gales of laughter.

"And this," she said, returning to her bag of gifts and drawing out the gourd dipper that I had requested to replicate a birth charm for the museum, "this has historical significance. Why, people used to eat their rice out of these. We did that when we visited my grandfather in the country."

"Historical significance," she had taken my words because they intrigued and pleased her. She has observed my life and now tells stories about Tallae's household as I tell stories about her telling stories.

Notes

Chapter One: The Storyteller

1. I have no objective proof that this was so, or that Yongsu's Mother benefited by my working with her. Elsewhere, anthropologists have noted where their presence enhanced a shaman's practice, family standing, or credit at local taverns (Binford 1980:14; Peters 1981:43).

2. Many of these objects are offerings presented to the shrine by clients. See Kendall 1985:54–56 for a more detailed description of Yongsu's Mother's shrine.

3. I am indebted to Roger Janelli for providing me with suitable words to describe what I saw.

4. David Mandelbaum suggests that many anthropologists write life history as a corrective to the ethnographic process whereby "dear friends have been dissolved into faceless norms; their vivid adventures . . . turned into pattern profiles or statistical types" (Mandelbaum 1973:178).

5. Films, on the other hand, transform a relatively anonymous encounter into a public event, even where some effort is made to conceal the informant's identity as in *Jero Tapakan.* The very process of filming can influence the performance of a life story (Connor, Asch, and Asch 1986:223–265).

6. Contemporary efforts to record otherwise unremarked-upon lives blend the interests and techniques of both anthropology and oral history. In American letters, the oral history of ordinary and often impoverished people began with the depression-era Federal Writers' Project of the Works Projects Administration (FWPWPA [1939] 1975). As a parallel but only recently convergent development, the anthropologist's life histories were initially collected to record the lifeways of vanishing people, then to explore their psyches on the basis of solid and comparable case material, and more recently to gain an intimate knowledge of perspectives, experiences, and feelings otherwise beyond

our ken. For a summary of the history, methods, and prospects of oral history, see Davis, Black, and MacLean 1977. See Brandes 1982, Langness and Frank 1981, and Watson and Watson-Franke 1985 for a similar accounting of life history.

With the development of women's studies, scholars now frequently address the necessity of recording women's lives lest we fail to comprehend the substance and variety of women's experiences (Geiger 1986; Sheridan and Salaff 1984), but note some thoughtful early remarks on this subject by Virginia Woolf ([1931] 1975).

7. See, for example, the behavior of the women at the Kim family *kut* (Kendall 1977) and the Chŏn family *kut* (Kendall 1985:1–22).

8. Case studies of shamans' lives are mustered to address the questions "how" and "why." How, through what manipulation of symbols and culturally validated experiences, is the initiate successfully transformed into a practicing shaman? Why is it that some social actors, but not others, experience possession trance? Among scholars who have addressed the "how" question, with varying degrees of awe and skepticism, are Eliade ([1951] 1970:33–144), Lebra (1969), Levi-Strauss (1963), Lewis (1969), and Peters (1981). For Korea, see Kim T. G. 1970, 1972, and Choi n.d.. For summaries of studies that address the "why" question by probing the cultural predispositions and psychological makeup of practicing shamans, see Fabrega 1974:32–39; Hippler 1976; Kennedy 1973; and Peters and Price-Williams 1980. For Korea, see Kim K. I. 1972 and Lee 1981. Harvey's work (1979, 1980) asks both how and why. For a range of portraits, see the Ministry of Culture's cumulative investigation of Korean folk belief (MCBCPP 1969–).

9. See for example, Harvey's study of women's experiences as adopted daughters-in-law *(minmyŏnŭri)* (Harvey 1983). Secreted away in the appendix of Cha-whan Chung's dissertation is the amazing picaresque portrait of a woman raised as an orphan, battered by various misadventures, but surviving (Chung 1977:207–222). See also my fictive mother's remembrance of her son's death (Kendall 1985:102–104).

Chapter Two: A Tale of Deceit and a Tale of Kam'ak Mountain

1. Affliction by invisible arrows is associated with transitional situations, births, weddings, and funerals. See Kendall 1985:105–107.

2. Although Hogu does not literally mean Princess, indeed the derivation is uncertain, *mansin* described Hogu to me as "like an old-fashioned princess." For more about Hogu, see Kendall 1985:13, 134–135, 138.

3. In planning a marriage, families rely on intelligence from a variety of sources. Relatives or friends in the prospective bride's or groom's community

will be consulted, and surreptitious scrutiny may be carried out under a variety of pretexts. Younghill Kang relates how his grandmother visited the bride's home disguised as an itinerant peddler (Kang [1931] 1959:45). In contemporary Korea, household registration and family records are accessible to public scrutiny; in combination, these documents provide information on family composition, ages, prior marital experience, and cohabitation. Some household ritual manuals include detailed instructions for do-it-yourself premarital investigations, and some detectives specialize in this service (Ko 1982:59–61). Investigations are particularly appropriate where the family relies on a professional matchmaker rather than a relative or friend.

4. By "bad fate," the elder sister refers to the "four pillars" *(saju),* the horoscopic properties of one's birth hour, day, month, and year. For a woman, "bad fate" usually means early widowhood, often a self-fulfilling prophecy insofar as such women are, like Yongsu's Mother, wed to older men. For discussions of divination and women's fate, see Janelli 1982; Kendall 1985:94–97; B. Young 1980, 1983.

5. Although one's personal fate may be overwhelmingly good, bad, or indifferent, it shifts in relation to the cycling of years, months, days, and hours. Year fate receives particular attention and the New Year is a busy season for diviners. The end of the year is considered an empty, neutral time.

6. Ch'un Hyang, the heroine of a popular tale, defies the lecherous advances of a corrupt magistrate and remains true to her sworn lover, who has gone to Seoul to sit for the civil service examination. Originally a long ballad opera *(p'ansori),* the story circulated as a vernacular novel and, in the modern era, has been perpetuated through such diverse media as movies and classics comic books. In the town of Namwŏn, tourists may visit "Ch'un Hyang's house," a thatched-roof cottage of recent construction. Holes poked in the door paper suggest eyes that have pried upon Ch'un Hyang's nuptial joys. Not this, but rather Ch'un Hyang's tribulations are evoked by Yongsu's Mother.

7. In this region it is customary that the bride's first meal in her husband's home should include squares of fried seaweed, consumed bundled around a lump of rice. But for this one festive touch, she describes a humble meal.

8. The bows that she describes constitute the *p'yebaek* ceremony, the final rite of a Korean wedding. The bride salutes all of her husband's kin who greet her as a new daughter-in-law. Raised in a relatively autonomous urban household, Yongsu's Mother was confounded by the traditional peasant community into which she had married. Members of her husband's surname group, the Yuns, lived together in the same hamlet and patterned their interactions on the basis of kinship. Old women addressed the youthful Yongsu's Mother as "grandmother" because she had married into a senior generation of the lineage. The solidarity and extensiveness of the Yun family is reflected in her wry comment, "I was dropping down to the floor and bobbing up all night."

9. A groom's unfastening of the long ribbon of his wife's jacket is a wedding night cliché. The bride is expected to turn her face demurely away and cast her eyes down in a final gesture of virginal modesty. A bold lass, indeed, slaps her husband's hand away.

10. Following a custom now supplanted by the honeymoon, the bride remained in the nuptial chamber for her first three days in her husband's house. It was considered shameful to leave the room, even to visit the outhouse, and brides ate and drank very little to avoid embarrassment. This accounts for some of Yongsu's Mother's reluctance to eat, even though she was ravenous. The three days in the inner room are matched by a similar period of seclusion, of longer duration, for a newborn baby and a woman who has just given birth; this is a period of liminality, of slow incorporation into the fabric of family life.

11. For a narrative description of a *kut,* see Kendall 1985, chap. 1; for more about flower-greeting *kut*, see Kendall 1985:81, 142–143.

12. Mountain Gods and their powers are described in Kendall 1985:esp. 128–131. Chung-moo Choi (personal communication) suggests that Yongsu's Mother's expression "use Kam'ak Mountain" *(sanŭl ssŭda)* may be idiosyncratic insofar as the phrase commonly means "to use a mountain for burial," another aspect of the mountain's liminality.

Chapter Three: Born in an Unlucky Hour

1. Korean floors, *ondol,* are heated by a system of flues; the hot spot, closest to the source of heat, is the place of honor.

2. Technically, *kisaeng* are equivalent to Japanese geisha, highly trained artists and companions. Yongsu's Mother uses the term more broadly to include all manner of hostesses, bar girls, and prostitutes. In this less restricted sense, venereal disease is sometimes called *"kisaeng pyŏng,"* the "*kisaeng* sickness."

3. Strangely, she uses the verb *taerida* instead of the honorific *mosida,* as though she were the adult (or superior) and her father were the child (or inferior).

4. See, for example, Harvey 1979:98, 100, 147–149; and Wilson 1983: 118.

5. For a discussion of adopted daughters-in-law, see Harvey 1983.

6. In addition to his kindness to Changmi, he financed the marriage of two co-workers, grateful that the intended groom would not reject a bride whose hand was mangled in one of the machines.

7. The Korean Youth League was the largest and most notorious antileftist youth group active between the Liberation and the Korean War (McCune 1950:162–163n, 228, 266).

Chapter Four: War Stories and a Meeting with the Mountain God

1. A good death is a death at home. Those who die violently, far from home, become restless, malevolent ghosts.

2. Bracketed ellipses mark the deletion of repetitive dialogue which makes for dramatic underscoring in oral performance but seemed tedious in print.

3. When I questioned her, she said that these events transpired just before the final retreat of the People's Army. Seoul was "neutralized" in early February of 1951 and retaken by U.N. troops in mid-March (Rees 1964).

4. Her mother recalls that, inspired by similar promises, groups of factory workers went north.

5. The only possible rival for frequency of recitation is the tale of the first wife's ghost, recounted in chapter 7.

6. One *mal* is the approximate equivalent of eighteen liters.

7. She uses the expression *wŏnhan,* the resentment and spite carried by a restless and consequently malevolent ghost (Kendall 1985:99–102).

8. The North Korean emblem adds a paintbrush to the hammer and sickle (Cumings 1984:52–53). The emblem that she describes is unknown to me, unless she misread the image on the bill.

9. The number of days varies slightly in the two accounts, possibly as a consequence of her disorientation in captivity.

10. The popular ballad tale of *Ch'un Hyang* contains a similar incident. The hero returns in rags and his mother-in-law does not recognize the identity of "me" (Rutt 1974:324).

11. His fears were reasonable since the city had changed hands four times.

12. See, for example, Ch'oe 1981:66–67; Harvey 1979:107, 153–154; Kim T. G. 1972; MCBCPP 1969:186–187. One of Choi's informants told her an almost identical story (Chung-moo Choi: personal communication).

13. Her reference to an active Youth League and to the "change of command" are strange if, as she claims, these events took place after the final retreat of the People's Army from Seoul in the spring of 1951.

14. In describing her activities as a member of the Youth League, she may be recalling events that transpired before the war (cf. McCune 1950:162–163n, 226, 228, 266).

Chapter Five: Buddha Ties

1. Body-Governing Gods (Momju) inspire shamans but, as personal spirits, they may also rise up and possess ordinary women when these women borrow the shamans' costumes and dance at *kut.* For more about the Body-Governing God, see Kendall 1984a and Kendall 1985:10–12, 16–17, 135–137, 142–143.

2. These sentiments are ironic insofar as the teachings and practices of Buddhism aim at transcending the appetites and longings that bind living and dead. This section illustrates the manner in which Korean folk religion, sometimes described as "Buddhism" (Pulgyo) by Yongsu's Mother and her clients, inverts Buddhist ideals by addressing the negative consequences of worldly craving.

3. I have condensed and rearranged a much longer statement.

4. The Hall of the Law (Pŏptang) is the main hall of a Buddhist temple, a term the *mansin* have borrowed to describe their own shrines.

5. Insofar as birth is considered a mildly polluting event, it seems strange that Yongsu's Grandmother should have given birth in a temple.

6. The Buddhist Sage is particularly strong in families where there have been pious women. For more about the Buddhist Sage, see Kendall 1985:131–133.

7. *Posal* literally means "bodhisattva"; temple caretakers are also called *posal,* but in this context it probably refers to an inspirational diviner. For more about *posal*, see Hardacre 1984:29–31; Kendall 1985:132; and Young 1980.

8. Yongsu's Mother uses the word "superstition" *(misin),* without its pejorative connotation, to designate the kinds of activities performed by shamans and their clients (Kendall 1985:28). That her mother "didn't even think about superstition" is an overstatement; she went for divinations and had even sponsored *kut.* What Yongsu's Mother suggests, as in her own story ("I was young; what did I know?"), is a deepening awareness and commitment validated in cumulative experiences.

9. That her brother alone was killed underscores the point of her tale, the power of the Buddhist Sage. Yongsu's Grandmother was more sanguine when she spoke to me of her son's death, acknowledging sadly that when young men were sent to the front with little training, of course they were slaughtered.

10. For more about the Seven Stars and their rituals, see Kendall 1985:80–81, 114, 116, 194n.3. For rituals of the New Year and first full moon, see Kendall 1985:74–76, 80, 141–142.

11. All of her currency references are with respect to 1977 prices and are stated as extremes of either miserliness or extravagance. At that time, five hundred won was the approximate equivalent of one U.S. dollar.

12. Among many other commodities, black market goods were a specialty of South Gate Market.

13. She refers to the prostitutes near American military encampments who serviced GIs. They are also known as *yang saeksi,* "Western miss," and *yang kongju,* "Western princess."

14. The Korean word *saeksi,* "Miss," was swiftly incorporated into the GI's camptown argot, probably because it sounds like the American colloquial "sexy."

15. "Babysan" is a transplant from the camptown argot of GIs stationed in Japan, as are "mamasan" and "moose" (*musume,* "daughter," "girl," "young lady").

16. See Kendall 1984a and Kendall 1985:4, 21, 66.

17. The relationship of a "spirit mother" and her apprentice "spirit daughter" is described in Kendall 1985:58–60, 68–67, 82, 133.

18. Again, I have condensed a long, repetitive introduction. The rest of the tale more nearly replicates her text.

19. Heretofore when she has told of carrying the Buddha away *(kajigo kada)* she has spoken of the image as an inanimate object. In direct address she expresses her intention to escort the Buddha *(mosigo kada)* as a respected being.

20. See, for example, Harvey 1979:65–67, 107–108, 152; Choi n.d.:101; Kim T. G. 1972:21; Ch'oe 1981:66–67.

21. Her son, Yongsu, had similar difficulties attending a Christian school (Kendall 1985:56–57).

22. The *hwan'gap,* marking the completion of a full cycle of life, is a major celebration and frequent excuse for a family reunion.

Chapter Six: The Reluctant Bride

1. In the 1980s it was common for a love match couple to pay their respects to both sets of parents and secure their blessing on the marriage. This was probably also Changmi's intention.

2. Shamans do comment on the compatibility of parental and fetal horoscopes, and some babies, like some brides, are believed to introduce good or bad fortune into the family. I have heard Yongsu's Mother encourage an ambivalent pregnant woman to keep a potentially lucky child, but not the reverse.

3. The ten-month pregnancy is reckoned from one month at conception.

4. See Kendall 1985:86–90 for a discussion of this ritual.

5. This would have been in 1960, when the Rhee government fell.

6. Today, the "first meeting" connotes a formal gathering of the two candidates, representatives of both families, and a matchmaker, who meet together in some neutral public place, usually a bakery or hotel coffee shop. The custom of first meetings became common over the last two decades. Initially, prospective grooms claimed the right to view and pass judgment on prospective brides, as in the case of Yongsu's Mother's marriage.

7. These are modern sentiments, widely accepted in the 1980s for both "love" and "match-made" marriages, but by no means universally acclaimed in the early 1960s, when Changmi's match was made.

8. See chap. 2, n. 2.

9. By custom, the married women of the household would "guard" the nuptial chamber, poking holes in the paper door and making their presence known, to the thorough embarrassment of an already bashful bride and groom.

10. I have consistently recorded this phrase as *mugamŭl ssŭda,* "use the *mugam.*" Chung-moo Choi (personal communication) suggests that the verb may rather be *sŭda,* Kyŏnggi dialect for *sŏda,* "to dance," thus "dance the *mugam.*"

11. See, for example, Casagrande 1960, and particularly Victor Turner's contribution. A very partial list of other works that provide sensitive descriptions of the anthropologist-informant relationship might include Clifford 1980; Crapanzano 1980; Dwyer 1982; Myerhoff 1978:esp. 40–78; Rabinow 1977; Shostak 1981; and Watson and Watson-Franke 1985:58–97. These varied accounts reveal that just as the emotional content of other diadic relationships varies with both personality and social expectation, the relationship of an anthropologist and his or her informant assumes many guises.

Chapter Seven: Old Ghosts and Ungrateful Children

1. For a description and analysis of *kosa,* see Kendall 1985:114–124.

2. For more about *yŏt'am,* see Kendall 1985:17, 33, 56, 135, 139.

3. The role of ghosts and ancestors in affliction is described in Kendall 1985:99–102, 150–160.

4. For an account of this incident, see Kendall 1985:56.

5. The stepdaughter's use of the term *sŏmo,* "father's concubine," rather than *kyemo,* "stepmother," underscores the insult. I am indebted to Chung-moo Choi for this distinction. See Kendall 1984b for a discussion of how, in some contexts, the second wife is perceived as a concubine.

6. This text followed the story of her marriage as told in chapter 2.

7. Although men perform the *chesa,* the day of an ancestral offering is particularly onerous for the women of the family who must prepare the offering food, the feast that will be served to all of the assembled family members, living and dead.

8. The members of *yangban* lineages were eligible to take the civil service examinations and hold public office. Those who claimed *yangban* ancestors constituted the rural local elite and saw themselves as the exemplars of Confucian social virtues.

9. The dawn *chesa* marked the end of the mourning period.

10. The A-frame carrier is a human beast of burden who receives small remuneration for transporting heavy loads on the pack frame he carries on his back.

11. Later she attributed her stomach trouble to wind *(param),* a chill humoral imbalance, but thought this also strange since she is careful to cover her middle regions with several layers of clothing. A few years later, after she had moved from the roadside house, she would note that water from the shallow well there had often made her ill. Her new house was equipped with an electric pump, raising pure water from a deep spring. For a more detailed account of how Yongsu's Mother dealt with her health problems, see Kendall n.d.b.

12. In the version of the tale told in 1985, her husband was too ashamed to tell the young wife of his dream. She heard it, roundabout, from a senior sister-in-law who confirmed the identity of the woman in Yongsu's Mother's own dreams.

13. For a discussion of the frequency with which dead first wives afflict living second wives, see Kendall 1984b.

14. This incident is described in Kendall 1985:62.

15. By my own interpretation, the dream distilled some of the contradictory emotions that I was experiencing after a year in the field. I was impatient to get on with things, with my own American life, and felt a bit guilty that this should be so. And yet, there were moments when I ached to be nothing so much as a competent village woman, anything but a bumbling and often tongue-tied anthropologist. I found in Yongsu's Mother's interpretation of my dream a comforting metaphor of acceptance.

Epilogue: 1985

1. The *kut* dialogue was taped but has been condensed. Most of the other quotations in this section are paraphrases culled from fieldnotes. Yongsu's Mother's remarks on marriage are a combination of two very similar conversations.

Glossary

Mansin and other Korean women learn the names of gods and rituals through oral transmission, and shaman chant books are in Korean script. Thus, many terms are ambiguous, with several possible interpretations, and the standard Chinese scholarly glosses employed in scholarly works seem to be educated guesses. In *Shamans, Housewives, and Other Restless Spirits* I cited etymologically intriguing cases in chapter notes. For consistency, I have continued to use the glosses adopted in this earlier work, favoring functional over literal interpretations. For example, here as there, Hogu is "the Princess" because the *mansin* describe her as "just like an old-fashioned princess." A single Chinese character is equivalent to a single syllabic cluster in *han'gul.*

anjŭn'gŏri mansin	앉은거리 만신 (萬神)	shaman who performs by chanting from a seated position
chaemi ŏptta	재미 없다	"no interest," unfavorable
Chagŭn Abŏji	작은 아버지	"little father," junior uncle
chesa	제사 (祭祀)	ritual offering to the ancestors
ch'isŏng tŭrida	치성 (致誠) 드리다	to make offerings to the spirits

ch'ŏtki	첫기 (…忌)	first anniversary of a death after a three-year mourning period
chubal	주발 (周鉢)	brass rice bowl
chuin	주인 (主人)	master, owner
Ch'ungch'ŏng (Province)	충청 (忠清)	
Ch'un Hyang	춘향 (春香)	"Spring Fragrance," heroine of a popular tale
geta (kyeda) (Japanese loan word)	げた (게다)	wooden-soled sandals
haejang kuk	해장국	tonic soup for hang-over
han	한 (恨)	grudge, grief of frustration and resentment
Hanyak	한약 (漢藥)	"Chinese Medicine," treatment with herbs, acupuncture, or moxibustion
hap	합 (盒)	lidded brass bowl
Hogu	호구 (戶口)	the Princess (god)
hongyŏk subi	홍역 (紅疫) 수비	measles' influences
hwan'gap	환갑 (還甲)	sixtieth birthday
Hyangt'o Yebigun	향토 예비군 (鄕土豫備軍)	Homeland Reserve
Imjin (River)	임진 (강) (臨津江)	
It'aewŏn (District)	이태원	
kaeksa	객사 (客死)	one who dies away from home
kajigo kada	가지고 가다	to take or carry with
Kam'ak/Kambak (Mountain)	감박 (산) (紺岳山)	
kisaeng	기생 (妓生)	female entertainer
kisaengbyŏng	기생병 (妓生病)	venereal disease

kkonmaji kut	꽃마지 굿	"flower-greeting *kut*" honoring the gods of a shrine or house
kosa	고사 (告祀)	ritual offering to the household gods
kunghap	궁합 (宮合)	divination to predict marital harmony
k'ŭnjip	큰집	big house, major line of descent
k'ŭn mansin	큰 만신 (萬神)	great shaman
k'ŭn paksa	큰 박사 (博士)	"great professor" (our joke)
kunung sal	군웅살 (軍雄煞)	invisible supernatural arrow
kut	굿	most elaborate shaman ritual
kwisin	귀신 (鬼神)	ghost/god
kwisin norŭm	귀신 (鬼神) 노름	ghostly play
kyemo	계모 (繼母)	stepmother
li *(ri)*	리 (里)	about one-third of a mile
mal	말	about eighteen liters
mama kut	마마 (媽媽) 굿	*kut* to appease the smallpox spirit
manse	만세 (萬歲)	"ten thousand years," thus "long live . . ."
mansin	만신 (萬神)	shaman
minmyŏnŭri	민며느리	daughter-in-law raised from childhood
Mirŭk	미륵 (彌勒)	Maitreya Buddha
Mirŭk Tang	미륵당 (彌勒堂)	Maitreya Shrine
misin	미신 (迷信)	"false belief," supersti-tion
Momju	몸주 (…主)	Body-Governing God

mosida	모시다	to accompany or serve a superior
mosigo kada	모시고 가다	to escort a superior
mudang	무당 (巫堂)	shaman or hereditary priestess
mudang sŏnsaeng	무당 선생 (巫堂 先生)	"shaman honorable teacher" (our joke)
mugam	무감 (巫…)	trance dance performed by ordinary women who wear the *mansin*'s costumes
Mulsin Halmŏni	물신 (…神) 할머니	Water Grandmother (god)
naerin saram	내린 사람	destined *mansin*
Namuamit'abul	나/남무아미타불 (南無阿彌陀佛)	invoking the name of Amida Buddha
nogu me	노구 메	rice offering to spirits
ondol	온돌 (溫突)	heated floor
paksa	박사 (博士)	professor
p'alcha	팔자 (八字)	the eight characters that determine one's fate
pan	반 (班)	administrative section of a neighborhood or village
pandong punja	반동 분자 (反動 分子)	reactionary element
Pangwigun	방위군 (防衛軍)	Defense Corps
panjang	반장 (班長)	neighborhood section chief
pan mudang	반 무당 (半 巫堂)	half shaman
p'ansori	판소리	solo ballad opera
param	바람	"wind," chill humoral imbalance

Pari Kongju	바리 공주 (鉢里 公主)	heroine of a shaman song performed during the *kut* for the dead
Pŏptang	법당 (法堂)	"Hall of the Law," main hall of Buddhist temple; shaman's shrine
posal	보살 (菩薩)	bodhisattva, title for temple caretaker or diviner
p'udakkŏri	푸닥거리	exorcism ritual
Pulgyo	불교 (佛教)	Buddhism
Pulsa	불사 (佛師/不死)	Buddhist Sage (god), or possibly Buddhist layperson who died while invoking the Buddha
p'yebaek	폐백 (幣帛)	bride's salutation to groom's family, final rite of Korean wedding
Pyŏlsang/-sŏng	별상/성 (别星)	Special Messenger (god)
sach'on	사촌 (四寸)	relatives to the fourth degree, cousins
saeksi	색시	young woman, miss
saju	사주 (四柱)	the "four pillars," horoscope determined by the year, month, day, and hour of birth
samch'on	삼촌 (三寸)	relatives to the third degree, uncles
Samgakchi (Intersection)	삼각지	
Sansin	산신 (山神)	Mountain God
Sinjang Momju	신장 (神將) 몸주 (…主)	Body-Governing Spirit Warrior

sinttal	신딸 (神…)	"spirit daughter," *mansin*'s apprentice
soju	소주 (燒酒)	crude vodka
sŏmo	서모 (庶母)	one's father's concubine
sŏng/hyŏng	성 / 형 (兄)	sibling, brother's wife
Sŏn Pawi	선 (仙) 바위	Immortal's Rock
sŏn poda	선 (先) 보다	to view potential bride or groom
sŏnsaeng	선생 (先生)	teacher
suyang ŏnni	수양 (収養) 언니	sworn sister
Taegam	대감 (大監)	Official (god)
Taehan Ch'ŏngnyŏndan	대한청년단 (大韓青年團)	Korean Youth League
taerida	대리다	to accompany or escort an equal or inferior
taesang	대상 (大祥)	final commemoration marking the end of mourning
Taesin Manura	대신 (大神) 마누라	consort of *mansin*'s guardian god
Taesin Sinjang	대신 신장 (大神 神將)	Great Spirit Warrior (Yongsu's Mother's guardian god)
tangju	당주 (堂主)	shrine keeper
tan'gol	단골 (丹骨)	regular client
Todang Halmŏni	도당 (都堂) 할머니	community Tutelary Grandmother (god)
todungnyŏ	도둑녀 (…女)	"robber woman"
tonghoe	동회 (洞會)	neighborhood association
tongjang	동장 (洞長)	neighborhood chiefs
Tongja Pyŏlsang/-sŏng	동자 별상 / 성 (童子 別星)	Child Messenger (god)

uni maegida 운 (運) 이매기다 to have one's fortune blocked or bound

wŏnhan 원한 (怨恨) resentment, grudge, spite

yaksu 약수 (藥水) medicinal water

yangban 양반 (兩班) high-born, hereditary elite

yang kalbo 양 (洋) 갈보 prostitutes servicing American GIs

yang kongju 양 공주 (洋公主) "Western princess"

yang saeksi 양 (洋) 색시 "Western miss"

yŏ-/yet'am 여 / 예탐 (豫探) feast food given to the ancestors before a wedding or *hwan'gap*

Bibliography

Agar, Michael. 1980. Hermeneutics in Anthropology: A Review Essay. *Ethos* 8:253–272.

Ardner, Edwin. 1972. Belief and the Problem of Women. In *The Intrepretation of Ritual,* ed. J. S. LaFontaine, 135–158. London: Tavistock.

Asch, Timothy, Linda Connor, and Patsy Asch. 1983. *Jero Tapakan: Stories from the Life of a Balinese Healer.* Watertown, Mass.: Documentary Educational Resources.

Bertaux-Wiame, Isabelle. 1981. The Life History Approach to the Study of Internal Migration. In *Bibliography and Society,* ed. D. Bertaux, 249–265. Beverly Hills: Sage Publications.

Binford, Martha B. 1980. Julia: An East African Diviner. In *Unspoken Worlds: Women's Religious Lives in Non-Western Cultures,* ed. N. A. Falk and R. M. Gross, 3–21. New York: Harper and Row.

Blackman, Margaret B. 1982. *During My Time: Florence Edenshaw Davidson, a Haida Woman.* Seattle: University of Washington Press.

Boas, Franz. 1943. Recent Anthropology. *Science* 98:334–337.

Brandes, Stanley. 1982. Ethnographic Autobiographies in American Anthropology. In *Crisis in Anthropology: View from Spring Hill, 1980,* ed. E. A. Hoebul, R. Currier, and S. Kaiser, 187–202. New York: Garland Publishers.

Casagrande, Joseph B., ed. 1960. *In the Company of Man: Twenty Portraits by Anthropologists.* New York: Harper Brothers.

Chamberlain, Mairy. [1975] 1983. *Fenwomen: A Portrait of Women in an English Village.* London: Routledge and Kegan Paul.

Ch'oe Kil-sŏng. 1981. *Han'guk musongnon* (Treatise on Korean shamanism). Seoul: Hyŏngsŏl Ch'ulp'ansa.

Choi, Chung-moo. n.d. The Creators of Destiny. MS.

Chung, Cha-whan. 1977. Change and Continuity in an Urbanizing Society: Family and Kinship in Urban Korea. Ph.D. diss., University of Hawaii.

Clark, Donald N. 1986. In the Eye of the Beholder: Women Missionaries' Views of Korean Women. Paper read at the thirty-eighth annual meeting of the Association for Asian Studies, Chicago, Illinois.

Clifford, James. 1980. Fieldwork, Reciprocity, and the Making of Ethnographic Texts: The Example of Maurice Leenhardt. *Man,* n.s. 15:518–532.

Connor, Linda, Patsy Asch, and Timothy Asch. 1986. *Jero Tapakan: Balinese Healer, an Ethnographic Film Monograph.* London: Cambridge University Press.

Cumings, Bruce. 1984. *The Two Koreas. Foreign Policy Association Headline Series,* no. 269.

Crapanzano, Vincent. 1977. Introduction. In *Case Studies in Spirit Possession,* ed. V. Crapanzano and V. Garrison, 1–40. New York: John Wiley.

———. 1980. *Tuhami: Portrait of a Moroccan.* Chicago: University of Chicago Press.

———. 1984. Life Histories (review essay). *American Anthropologist* 86 (4):953–960.

Davis, Cullon, Kathryn Black, and Kay MacLean. 1977. *Oral History: From Tape to Type.* Chicago: American Library Association.

Dwyer, Kevin. 1982. *Moroccan Dialogues: Anthropology in Question.* Baltimore: Johns Hopkins University Press.

Eliade, Mircea. [1951] 1970. *Shamanism: Archaic Techniques of Ecstasy.* Trans. R. W. Trask. New York: Pantheon Books.

Fabrega, Horatio. 1974. *Disease and Social Behavior: An Interdisciplinary Perspective.* Stanford: Stanford University Press.

Federal Writers' Project of the Works Progress Administration in North Carolina, Tennessee, and Georgia (FWPWPA). [1939] 1975. *These Are Our Lives.* New York: W. W. Norton.

Frank, Gelya. 1979. Finding the Common Denominator: A Phenomenological Critique of Life History Method. *Ethos* 7:69–94.

Freeman, James, and David L. Krantz. 1979. The Unfulfilled Promise of Life Histories. *Biography* 3:1–13.

Geiger, Susan N. G. 1986. Women's Life Histories: Method and Content (review essay). *Signs* 11:334–351.

Haboush, JaHyun Kim. 1986. Multiple Loyalties: A Life of a Royal Woman. Paper read at thirty-eighth annual meeting of the Association for Asian Studies, Chicago, Illinois.

Han, Chungnim C. 1949. The Social Organization of Upper Han Hamlet. Ph.D. diss., University of Michigan.

Hardacre, Helen. 1984. *The Religion of Japan's Korean Minority: The Preservation of Ethnic Identity.* Korea Research Monograph 9. Berkeley: University of California, Institute for East Asian Studies.

Harvey, Youngsook Kim. 1979. *Six Korean Women: The Socialization of Shamans.* Saint Paul: West Publishing.

———. 1980. Possession Sickness and Women Shamans in Korea. In *Unspoken Worlds: Women's Religious Lives in Non-Western Cultures,* ed. N. A. Falk and R. M. Gross, 31–52. New York: Harper and Row.

———. 1983. *Minmyŏnŭri:* The Daughter-in-law Who Comes of Age in Her Mother-in-law's Household. In *Korean Women: A View from the Inner Room,* ed. L. Kendall and M. Peterson, 45–61. New Haven: East Rock Press.

Hippler, A. E. 1976. Shamans, Curers, and Personality: Suggestions toward a Theoretical Model. In *Culture-bound Syndromes, Ethnopsychiatry, and Alternative Therapies,* ed. W. P. Lebra, 103–114. Honolulu: University of Hawaii Press.

Janelli, Dawnhee Yim. 1982. Faith, Fortunetelling, and Social Failure. In *Religions in Korea: Beliefs and Cultural Values,* ed. E. H. Phillips and E. Y. Yu, 59–69. Los Angeles: Center for Korean and Korean-American Studies, California State University, Los Angeles.

Janelli, Roger L., and Dawnhee Yim Janelli. 1982. *Ancestor Worship and Korean Society.* Stanford: Stanford University Press.

Kang, Younghill. [1931] 1959. *The Grass Roof.* Chicago: Follet Publishing.

Keesing, Roger M. 1985. Kwaio Women Speak: The Micro-politics of Autobiography in a Solomon Island Society. *American Anthropologist* 87:27–39.

Kendall, Laurel. 1977. Caught between Ancestors and Spirits: A Korean *Mansin*'s Healing *Kut. Korea Journal* 17 (8):8–23.

———. 1984a. Giving Rise to Dancing Spirits: *Mugam* in Korean Shaman Ritual. In *Dance as Cultural Heritage,* vol. 1, ed. B. T. Jones, 224–232. *Dance Research Annual,* no. 14.

———. 1984b. Wives, Lesser Wives, and Ghosts: Supernatural Conflict in a Korean Village. *Asian Folklore Studies* (Nagoya) 43 (2):215–225.

———. 1985. *Shamans, Housewives, and Other Restless Spirits: Women in Korean Ritual Life.* Honolulu: University of Hawaii Press.

———. n.d.a. Cold Wombs *(Naeng)* in Balmy Honolulu: A Korean Illness Category in Translation. Forthcoming in *Social Science and Medicine.*

———. n.d.b. Healing Thyself: A Korean Shaman's Afflictions. Forthcoming in *Social Science and Medicine.*

Kendall, Laurel, and Mark Peterson. 1983. "Traditional Korean Women": A Reconsideration. In *Korean Women: A View from the Inner Room,* ed. L. Kendall and M. Peterson, 5–21. New Haven: East Rock Press.

Kennedy, John G. 1973. Cultural Psychiatry. In *Handbook of Social and Cultural Anthropology,* ed. J. Honigman, 1149–1152. Chicago: Rand McNally.

Kim, Kwang-iel [Kim Kwang-il]. 1972. Sin-byŏng: A Culture-bound Depersonalization Syndrome in Korea. *Neuropsychiatry* (Seoul) 11:223–234.

Kim T'ae-gon. 1966. *Hwangch'on muga yŏngu* (A study of shaman songs of the yellow springs). Seoul: Institute for the Study of Indigenous Religion.

———. 1970. A Study of Shaman's Mystic Illness during Initiation Process in Korea. *Journal of Asian Women* (Seoul) 9:91–132.

———. 1972. Components of Korean Shamanism. *Korea Journal* 12 (12):17–25.

Kluckhohn, Clyde. 1945. The Personal Document in Anthropological Science. In *The Use of Personal Documents in History, Anthropology, and Sociology,* ed. L. Gottschalk, C. Kluckhohn, and R. Angell. *Social Science Research Council Bulletin* 53:78–173.

Ko Chŏng-gi. 1982. *Algi Swiun Kwanhonsangje* (Passage rites made easy). Seoul: Huri Ch'ulp'ansa.

Langness, L. L. 1965. *The Life History in Anthropological Science.* New York: Holt, Rinehart, and Winston.

Langness, L. L., and Gelya Frank. 1981. *Lives: An Anthropological Approach to Biography.* Novato, Calif.: Chandler and Sharp.

Lebra, Takie Sugiyama. 1984. *Japanese Women: Constraint and Fulfillment.* Honolulu: University of Hawaii Press.

Lebra, William P. 1966. *Okinawan Religion: Belief, Ritual, and Social Structure.* Honolulu: University of Hawaii Press.

———. 1969. Shaman and Client in Okinawa. In *Mental Health Research in Asia and the Pacific,* ed. W. Caudill and J. Y. Lin, 216–222. Honolulu: East-West Center Press.

Lee, Jung-young. 1981. *Korean Shamanistic Rituals.* The Hague: Mouton.

Levi-Strauss, Claude. 1963. The Sorcerer and His Magic. In *Structural Anthropology,* trans. C. Jacobson and B. Schaepf, 167–185. New York: Basic Books.

Lewis, I. M. 1966. Spirit Possession and Deprivation Cults. *Man,* n.s. 1 (3):307–329.

———. 1969. *Ecstatic Religion.* Harmondsworth: Penguin.

Lewis, Oscar. 1963. *The Children of Sanchez: Autobiography of a Mexican Family.* New York: Vintage.

Little, Kenneth. 1980. Explorations and Individual Lives: A Reconsideration of Life Writing in Anthropology. *Dialectical Anthropology:* 210–226.

McCune, George M. 1950. *Korea Today.* Cambridge: Harvard University Press.

Mandelbaum, David. 1973. The Study of Life History: Gandhi. *Current Anthropology* 14:177–206.

Marcus, George E., and Dick Cushman. 1982. Ethnographies as Texts. *Annual Review of Anthropology 1982* 11:25–69.

Ministry of Culture and Bureau of Cultural Properties Preservation (MCBCPP). 1969–. *Han'guk minsok chonghap chosa pogosŏ* (Report on the cumulative investigation of Korean folk belief). Cum. vols. arranged by province. Seoul: Ministry of Culture, Bureau of Cultural Properties Preservation.

Mintz, Sidney W. 1974. *Worker in the Cane.* New York: W. W. Norton.

Myerhoff, Barbara. 1978. *Number Our Days.* New York: Simon and Schuster.

Myerhoff, Barbara, and Jay Ruby. 1982. Introduction. In *A Crack in the Mirror: Reflexive Perspectives in Anthropology,* ed. J. Ruby, 1–35. Philadelphia: University of Pennsylvania Press.

Obeyesekre, Gananath. 1981. *Medusa's Hair: An Essay on Personal Symbols and Religious Experience.* Chicago: University of Chicago Press.

Peters, Larry. 1981. *Ecstasy and Healing in Nepal: An Ethnopsychiatric Study of Tamang Shamanism.* Malibu: Uneda Publications.

Peters, Larry, and Douglas Price-Williams. 1980. Toward an Experiential Analysis of Shamanism. *American Ethnologist* 7:397–419.

Rabinow, Paul. 1977. *Reflections on Fieldwork in Morocco.* Berkeley and Los Angeles: University of California Press.

Rees, David. 1964. *Korea: The Limited War.* London: Macmillan.

Riley and Schram. 1951. *The Reds Take a City: The Communist Occupation of Seoul with Eyewitness Accounts.* New Brunswick: Rutgers University Press.

Rosaldo, Renato. 1976. The Story of Tukbaw: "They Listen as He Orates." In *The Biographical Process: Studies in the History of Psychology of Religion,* ed. F. E. Reynolds and D. Capps, 121–151. The Hague: Mouton.

Rutt, Richard. 1974. The Song of a Faithful Wife, Ch'unhyang. In *Virtuous Women: Three Classic Korean Novels,* trans. R. Rutt and C. Kim, 250–333. Seoul: Royal Asiatic Society Press.

Sharon, Douglas. 1978. *Wizard of the Four Winds: A Shaman's Story.* London: The Free Press.

Sheridan, Mary, and Janet W. Salaff, eds. 1984. *Lives: Chinese Working Women.* Bloomington: Indiana University Press.

Shostak, Marjorie. 1981. *Nisa: The Life and Words of a !Kung Woman.* Cambridge: Harvard University Press.

Turner, Victor W. 1960. Muchonga the Hornet, Interpreter of Religion. In *In the Company of Man: Twenty Portraits by Anthropologists,* ed. J. Casagrande, 333–355. New York: Harper and Brothers.

Watson, Lawrence C. 1976. Understanding a Life History as a Subjective

Document: Hermeneutical and Phenomenological Perspectives. *Ethos* 4:95–131.

Watson, Lawrence C., and Maria Barbara Watson-Franke. 1985. *Interpreting Life Histories.* New Brunswick, N.J.: Rutgers University Press.

Wilson, Brian. 1983. The Korean Shaman: Image and Reality. In *Korean Women: A View from the Inner Room,* ed. L. Kendall and M. Peterson, 113–126. New Haven: East Rock Press.

Woolf, Virginia. [1931] 1975. Introductory Letter to Margaret Lewelyn Davies. In *Life as We Have Known It, by Co-operative Working Women,* ed. M. L. Davies, xv–xxix. New York: Norton Library.

Young, Barbara. 1980. Spirits and Other Signs: An Ethnography of Divination in Seoul, R.O.K. Ph.D. diss., University of Washington.

———. 1983. City Women and Divination: Signs in Seoul. In *Korean Women: View from the Inner Room,* ed. L. Kendall and M. Peterson, 139–157. New Haven: East Rock Press.

Young, Michael. 1983. "Our Name Is Women: We Are Bought with Limesticks and Limepots": An Analysis of the Autobiographical Narrative of a Kalauna Woman. *Man,* n.s. (18) 3:478–501.

Zampleni, Andras. 1977. From Symptom to Sacrifice: The Story of Khady Fall. In *Case Studies in Spirit Possession,* ed. V. Crapanzano and V. Garrison, 87–139. New York: John Wiley.

Index

Abortion, 87, 88–89, 91
American soldiers, 66, 71–72, 134nn.13, 14, 135n.15
Ancestors, restless, 103, 117. *See also* Dead, the; Ghosts
Ancestor worship, 6–7, 8. See also *Chesa*
Anthropologist-informant relationship: and academic analogy, 2–3, 37; and collaboration, 99–100, 126–127; descriptions of, 136n.11; and friendship, 121; interpretive challenges of, 12–13; legitimizing shaman's occupation, 64, 129n.1
Anticommunism, 54
Asch, Patsy, 9
Asch, Timothy, 9
Auspicious dates, 22, 124. *See also* Horoscope
Avoidance, 107

Birth: of elder brother, 69; of Willow Market Daughter, 10, 91–93. *See also* Childbirth
Body-Governing God (Momju), 3, 68, 90, 133n.1
Body-Governing Spirit Warrior (Sinjang Momju), 120, 121
Boil Face Mansin, 87, 91–92
Brass Mirror Mansin, 5
Bride: dress of, 22, 96, 108; first meal of, 23–24, 131n.7; maiden as, 28; seclusion of, 25, 132n.10
Buddha statue, little, 3, 10, 75–78, 80, 135n.19
Buddhism, 6, 68–69, 123, 134n.2
Buddhist Sage, 68, 69, 79–80, 134nn.6, 9
Burial, 90

Changmi. *See* Yongsu's Mother
Chatterbox Mansin (elder sister): gods of, 63, 123–124; and little Buddha statue, 76–77; *kut* of, 77, 98; as matchmaker, 87, 94; retirement of, 123, 125; and Yongsu's Mother, 20, 21–22, 23, 28, 45, 116, 117
Chesa, 105, 106, 136nn.7, 9. *See also* Ancestor worship
Childbirth, 10, 69, 91–93, 132n.10, 134n.5
Childcare, 33, 34–37, 41–43, 50
Child labor, 36–37, 45–46, 71–72
Child Messengers (Tongja Pyŏlsang), 116
Chinese medicine, 89, 92, 111, 112
Ch'oe, Kil-song, 16
Choi, Chung-moo, 132n.12, 133n.12, 136nn.5, 10
Christianity, 29, 81, 125
Chung, Cha-whan, 130n.9
Ch'ungch'ŏng Province, 73
Ch'un Hyang, 23, 131n.6, 133n.10
Clear Spring Mansin, 116, 117
Clientele, of Yongsu's Mother, 6, 122–123
Concubines, 19, 44, 136n.5. *See also* Little mother
Confucianism, 136n.8
Connor, Linda, 9
Courtship, 85–86
Crapanzano, Vincent, 13, 14

Dance, 80–81, 98–99, 133n.1
Dating, 125
Daughter-in-law: adopted, 44, 130n.9, 132n.5; trouble with, 27, 71, 116–117, 125, 126

Dead, the: danger of, 8, 101–103, 111–115, 116; exorcism of, 119; as shrine spirit, 102. *See also* Ghosts
Death: of brothers, 32, 70; of father, 84, 89–90; of first wife, 114; a good, 133n.1; of husband, 98, 112–113; of little sister, 19; and taboo, 28
Death anniversary, 3, 31, 98
Defense Corps (Pangwigun), 64
Devil possession, 1
Divination: for illness, 72, 84, 110; manual of, 37; for misfortune, 7, 102; at New Year, 119, 131n.5; and pregnancy, 87. *See also* Dreams; Horoscope
Dowry, 99
Dreams: interpretation of, 116, 117, 118, 123, 137n.15; of Kendall, 118, 137n.15; of Yongsu's Mother, 73, 74–76, 79–80, 102, 109, 113, 115–116, 117, 123; of Yongsu's Mother's husband, 111–112, 137n.12; of Yongsu's Mother's mother, 69; of Yongsu's Mother's sister-in-law, 98, 114
Dress, proper, 124
Drinking: and Yongsu's Mother's father, 34, 40; and Yongsu's Mother's husband, 19, 30, 105, 106–107, 112, 120, 121; and Yongsu's Mother's lover, 89
Drumming, 73

Economy, of Enduring Pine Village, 5
Edel, Leon, 101
Education, 34–37, 38, 45, 123
Elder brother, 34, 40–41, 43, 69, 70
Elder sister. *See* Chatterbox Mansin
Enduring Pine Village, 5, 31
Engagement party, 99
Exorcism, 7, 92, 103, 109, 110, 117

Family history, 8, 44
Fate: bad, 131n.4; of Yongsu's Mother, 3, 10, 16, 21, 31–32, 63, 81, 98
Father-daughter relationship, 38
Federal Writers' Project of Works Projects Administration, 129n.6
Film, 9, 129n.5
First meeting, of marriage candidates, 93–94, 135n.6
First wife: dead, 137n.13; of Yongsu's Mother's husband, 103, 109, 112–113, 114–115
Folk religion, 134n.2
Food: at bride's first meal, 24–25, 131n.7; at family meals, 39; for funeral, 84; in Korean War, 47–50, 51, 64–65. *See also* Hunger
Four pillars *(saju)*, 131n.4
Funeral, 84, 89–90

Ghosts: ancestors as, 91, 117, 133n.1; exorcism of, 115, 119; and illness, 92; nature of, 102, 133n.7; Yongsu's Mother as, 60. *See also* Dead, the
Gift exchange: 22, 25, 95, 99, 127
Gods: descent of, 63, 77, 79, 98; household, 7–8; sex of, 122; and shamans, 62–64. See also *names of individual gods*
Grandfather: and shrine, 121; sixtieth birthday for, 82–83; and Yongsu's Mother's escape from Peoples' Army, 53, 58–59; as Yongsu's Mother's protective deity, 56, 57, 73, 75–76, 77, 80, 98, 116. *See also* Mountain Gods
Grandmother, 77, 118; in Yongsu's Mother's dreams, 73, 75–76, 79–80, 123
Great Spirit Grandmother, 123
Great Spirit Warrior (Taesin Sinjang), 120, 121
Great Spirit Wife (Taesin Manura), 124

Hall of the Law (Pŏptang), 134n.4
Hallucinations, 74–75
Han, 8
Han River Bridge, 69
Harvey, Youngsook Kim, 11–12, 16, 38, 79, 130nn.8, 9
Hermeneutics, 13
Homeland Reserve (Hyangt'o Yebigun), 43, 64
Horoscope: and fate, 131nn.4, 5; of fetus, 135n.2; and marriage, 22, 37, 96; of Yongsu's Mother, 31–32. *See also* Divination; Fate
Hospital: and Yongsu's Mother, 89, 92; and Yongsu's Mother's father, 83; and Yongsu's Mother's husband, 107, 112, 113; and Yongsu's Mother's stepson, 109, 111
House, 5–6, 23, 112
Household: expenses of, 39, 41, 42, 43, 48; religious life of, 8

Hunger, 47–50, 51, 52–53, 55–57, 67, 71. *See also* Food
Husband. *See* Yongsu's Mother's husband
Hwan'gap. *See* Sixtieth birthday

Illness: and the dead, 8, 92; divination for, 72, 84, 98; exorcism of, 7, 109, 110; *kut* for, 75–76, 109; measles, 32, 33, 109–111; smallpox, 19, 115–116; of Yongsu's Mother, 91–92, 98, 137n.11
Imjin River, 22, 55, 96
Immigration, 125
Immortal's Rock (Sŏn Pawi), 73, 117
Informants, 13–14. *See also* Anthropologist-informant relationship
Invisible arrow *(kunung sal),* 19, 130n.1

Jade Immortal, 123
Janelli, Roger, 129n.3
Jero Tapakan: Stories from the Life of a Balinese Healer, 9, 129n.5

Kam'ak Mountain, 28–30, 63, 132n.12
Kin, protection of, 44
Kisaeng, 132n.2
Korean War, 10, 43, 47–50
Korean Youth League (Taehan Ch'ŏngnyŏndan): described, 132n.7; feeding Seoul elderly, 64–65; and reds, 47, 54, 65–66; and Yongsu's Mother, 46, 51, 69, 133nn.13, 14
Kosa, 101, 136n.1
Kunghap, 37
Kut: busy season for, 101; for the dead, 33; and family history, 8; flower-greeting *(kkonmaji kut),* 28, 31, 68, 115, 122, 132n.11; gods at, 79, 90, 120–121; for illness, 19, 72–73, 75–76, 84, 92, 109, 112; reasons for, 7, 31, 115; and shaman's performance, 6

Lewis, Oscar, 13, 14
Liberation Day, 46
Life histories: and anthropology, 4, 8, 11–15, 129nn.4, 6; and film, 129n.5; methodology of, 10; of shamans, 16, 130n.8
Little mother, 42–45, 48, 49–50, 82, 83

Maitreya Shrine (Mirŭk Tang), 76, 77
Mandelbaum, David, 129n.4
Mansin: anjŭn'gori, 72–73; busy season of, 101; and divination, 102; gender of, 6; as informants, 16; *tan'gol,* 7. *See also* Shamans
Marriage: first meeting of candidates, 135n.6; and gift exchange, 95, 99; Korean views of, 91, 127; and *mansin,* 121–122; and prenuptial investigations, 86, 87, 88; of Yongsu's Mother, 19–25, 93–97
Matchmaker, 19, 21, 94, 131n.3, 135n.6 *See also* Prenuptial investigations
Measles, 32, 33, 109–111
Methodology, of this study, 2–4, 9–11, 14–15, 18, 54–55, 91, 99–100, 126–127, 137n.1
Migrants, 44
Money: and household expenses, 41, 42; and illness, 83–84, 110; and *kut,* 84, 99; and marriage, 83, 95, 122; People's Army, 56, 66; and ritual observances, 69; and school, 35
Mother-in-law, 117. *See also* Daughter-in-law
Mountain, ritual use of, 76, 117, 119, 122. *See also* Kam'ak Mountain
Mountain Gods, 8, 54, 63, 132n.12; and Yongsu's Mother, 3, 28, 30, 56, 57, 58–59, 62–64, 80, 98
Mourning, 90, 98, 105
Mugam, 98

Namsan Mansin, 12
National Army, 49, 51, 52, 60–61, 65
Neighborhood association *(tonghoe),* 66
Neighborhood chiefs *(panjang),* 45, 65, 66
New Year, 7, 31, 118, 131n.5, 134n.10
Noxious influences, 119
Nuptial chamber, 97–98, 136n.9

Occupations: of women, 44, 45, 66; of Yongsu's Mother, 44, 45–46, 71–72, 98; of Yongsu's Mother's parents, 34
Offerings: to ancestors, 101–102; for illness, 75, 76, 77, 98, 110; at New Years, 118–119; occasions for, 69, 70; to Seven Stars, 124; and shrines, 78, 121, 129n.2. See also *Chesa; Yŏt'am* offerings
Okhwa, 105–107, 108

Okkyŏng's Mother, 102, 103, 120, 122
Oral history, 129n.6

People's Army: and capture of Yongsu's Mother, 10, 51–62, 64, 76; retreat of, 133nn.3, 13; in Seoul, 48, 49, 65
Performance: and *kut,* 6–7, 19, 68, 120–121; and storytelling, 14; and Yongsu's Mother, 9
Phenomenology, 13
Phillips, Herbert, 14
Pilgrimage, mountain, 3, 122
Pollution, 98, 117, 134n.5. *See also* Taboo
Posal, 112, 134n.7
Pregnancy, 37, 86–87, 88, 89, 135n.3
Prenuptial investigations, 19, 22, 86, 87, 88, 95, 130n.3
Princess (Hogu), 19, 130n.2
Princess Pari, 33, 54
Prostitutes, 50–51, 71–72, 132n.2, 134n.13
Purification rites, 28, 117
P'yebaek ceremony, 131n.8
Pyŏngyang Mansin, 12, 79

Rationing, 66–67
Refugees, 58
Remarriage, 102, 116
Ritual manuals, 37, 131n.3

Seoul, 60–62, 133n.3
Seven Stars, 8, 70, 124, 134n.10
Sex roles: in courtship, 85–86; and education, 34–35, 45; and life histories, 13, 15–16; in ritual, 6–7, 8, 136n.7; and shamanism, 6–7
Shaman: destined, 62–64, 79, 81, 98; and divination, 110; gender of, 6; legitimizing of, 79–80; life histories of, 16, 130n.8; status of, 79. See also *Mansin*
Shamans, Housewives, and Other Restless Spirits, 8–9
Shostak, Marjorie, 13, 14
Shrine: of Chatterbox Mansin, 78; of offering at, 75–76, 98; village, 117–119; of Yongsu's Mother, 1, 5–6, 120–121, 123
Siblings, of Yongsu's Mother, 19, 32, 69–71. *See also* Chatterbox Mansin; Elder brother; Tong-gil
Sister-in-law, 106
Six Korean Women: The Socialization of Shamans, 11–12, 16
Sixtieth birthday *(hwan'gap),* 45, 81–83, 135n.22
Smallpox, 19, 115–116
Songjuk Mansin, 121–122, 123, 127
Sons, 28–29, 32–33, 70–71
Special Messenger (Pyŏlsang), 19, 116
Spirit clothes, 102, 124
Spirit daughter *(sin ttal),* 73, 87, 135n.17
Spirit Warrior, 6, 99, 102
Squatter Shack Mansin, 75
Stepchildren, 18, 25, 29, 104–105, 109
Stepdaughter, 25, 104–105. *See also* Okhwa
Stepmother, problems of, 104–105, 109
Stepson, 18, 109–111
Storytellers, 13–14
Storytelling, 9. *See also* Performance
Suwŏn Mansin, 16

Taboo, 19, 28
Tale of Princess Pari (Pari Kongju), 33
Tape recorder, use of, 4, 9, 54, 126, 137n.1
Teacher, 36, 37, 78
Television, 5, 54, 122
Tong-gil, 61, 82, 83, 90

United States, 125, 126–127. *See also* American soldiers

Village Shrine Grandmother (Todang Halmŏni), 118
Violence: of Korean Youth League, 65–66; of People's Army, 52–53; of Yongsu's Mother's father, 34–37, 41, 42–43, 50, 85–86; of Yongsu's Mother's husband, 107; of Yongsu's Mother's lover, 89, 90

Water, medicinal *(yaksu),* 73, 75–76, 79
Water Grandmother (Mulsin Halmoni), 28
Wedding: auspicious date for, 22; and *p'ybaek* ceremony, 131n.8; and feast, 97–98; journey of Yongsu's Mother, 22–23, 96–97; night, 24–25, 132n.9, 136n.9
Widower: Yongsu's Mother's husband as, 114–115; Yun, 27, 116

Widowhood: as bad fate, 131n.4; of Yongsu's Mother, 30, 44, 114–115, 122–123
Willow Market Daughter, 10, 37–38, 86–87, 91, 122
Wilson, Brian, 16
Women: and the dead, 8; education of, 34–35, 45; and life histories, 13, 15–16, 130n.6; occupations of, 34, 44, 45, 66. *See also* Sex roles
Woolf, Virginia, 1

Yangban, 106, 120, 124, 136n.8
Yongsu, 123, 125, 126
Yongsu's Mother: appearance of, 6, 15; and American soldiers, 71–72; and Buddha statue, 75–78; and Chatterbox Mansin, 20–22, 23, 28, 45, 76–78, 87, 94, 98, 116, 117, 123–124; childhood of, 32, 34–37; dreams of, 74–76, 79–80, 102, 113, 115–116, 117; education of, 34–37; fate of, 3, 10, 16, 21, 31–32, 63, 81, 98; and elder brother, 51, 52; and father, 18–19, 38–43, 48–50; and the gods, 62–64, 77, 79–80, 120–121; house of, 5–6, 122; and husband, 19, 20–21, 31, 112–113; and illness, 72–73, 91–92, 137n.11; in Korean Youth League, 46; little sister of, 19; marriage of, 19–27, 96–97; occupations of, 36–37, 45–46, 71–72, 80; and People's Army, 49, 51–54, 55–62, 64–66; shrine of, 1, 5–6, 123; as stepmother, 18, 25, 104–109; as storyteller, 9–10, 26; success of, 6, 122–123
Yongsu's Mother's father: betrayal of, 48–50, 82–84; death of, 84, 89–90; in dream, 117; drinking of, 34, 40; occupation of, 34; second family of, 39–41; violence of, 34–37, 41, 42–43, 50, 85–86
Yongsu's Mother's husband: and death, 31, 101–102; drinking of, 19, 30, 105, 106–107, 112, 120, 121; first meeting with, 20–21; illness of, 112–113
Yongsu's Mother's mother: as adopted daughter-in-law, 44; Body-Governing God of, 68, 90; and little mother, 45, 50; occupation of, 34
Yŏt'am offerings, 101–102, 115, 136n.2
Yun, widower, 116
Yun family, 28–30, 131n.8

HAWAII **Production Notes**

This book was designed by Roger Eggers. Composition and paging were done on the Quadex Composing System and typesetting on the Compugraphic 8400 by the design and production staff of University of Hawaii Press.

The text and display typeface is Sabon.

Offset presswork and binding were done by Vail-Ballou Press, Inc. Text paper is Glatfelter Offset Vellum, basis 50.